Clinician's Guide to

Getting Better Bit(e) By Bit(e)

Clinician's Guide
to
Getting Better
Bit(e) by Bit(e)

A Survival Kit for Sufferers of Bulimia
Nervosa and Binge Eating
Disorders

Janet Treasure

and

Ulrike Schmidt

Institute of Psychiatry
London, UK

Routledge
Taylor & Francis Group

LONDON AND NEW YORK

First published 1997 by Routledge
27 Church Road, Hove, East Sussex BN3 2FA

Simultaneously published in the USA and Canada
by Routledge
270 Madison Avenue, New York NY 10016

Reprinted 1998, 2003 and 2006

Routledge is an imprint of the Taylor & Francis Group, an informa business

© 1997 Routledge

British Library Cataloguing in Publication Data
A catalogue record for this book is available from the British Library

  ISBN 13: 978-0-86377-730-1 (hbk)
  ISBN 10: 0-86377-730-9 (hbk)

Printed and bound in the UK by TJ International (Padstow) Ltd
This publication has been produced with paper manufactured to strict environmental standards and with pulp derived from sustainable forests.

Acknowledgements

We are deeply indebted to William Miller, who has trodden the same path, albeit in a different context. We started in the field from a different direction, but the problems and solutions that he had found meant that our paths crossed. We adapted "motivational enhancement therapy" for use with bulimia nervosa. Most of the principles are the same as those that he and his colleagues developed for use with people with alcohol and drug problems. He is an inspiring, overt and covert, teacher and clinician. We also wish to sincerely thank Steve Rollnick for his role in training us in the principles of motivational interviewing. This is the oil which eases the movement of change.

Our special thanks go to Tom Treasure, who contributed the cartoons. Jane Tiller and Joey Loessem kindly supplied us with some of the case vignettes. Dave Attwell, Kate Trotter, Becky Trowler, and Nick Troop made helpful comments on the manuscript. We gratefully acknowledge the help of Janice May in preparing the manuscript.

The development of this work sprang from the ideas and leadership of Professor Gerald Russell. It has been enriched and expanded by the teaching and writing of William Miller and Steve Rollnick who introduced us to the spirit of change.

All royalties from this book will go to the Eating Disorder Research Fund of the Institute of Psychiatry.

Last, but not least, we would like to acknowledge our patients, many of whose comments and ideas were invaluable in developing this book.

Contents

Appendix: Workbook—Motivational Enhancement Therapy

Getting Better Bit(e) by Bit(e)
A Survival Kit for Sufferers of Bulimia Nervosa and Binge Eating Disorders

Introduction

Clinician's Guide
to
Getting Better Bit(e) by Bit(e)

INTRODUCTION

After the publication of our self-help book *Getting Better Bit(e) by Bit(e): A Survival Kit for Sufferers of Bulimia Nervosa and Binge Eating Disorders*, we were approached by several therapists who told us that they used *Bit(e) by Bit(e)* as a basis of their treatment. We also were using it in our practice. We were therefore interested in finding the optimal method of training our colleagues so that they could use it as part of guided self-care.

The research we had done using the book gave us lots of ideas. With the help of the Mental Health Foundation and the British Council we investigated the effectiveness of *Bit(e) by Bit(e)*. We found that approximately 1 in 5 people with bulimia nervosa could benefit from the manual alone. Another 2 out of 5 benefited if the manual is given in conjunction with therapy.

One of the main factors that limited the use of the manual in our study was poor compliance. For example, only 6 out of 10 people given the book read more than half of it. Only 5 out of 10 people completed 3 or more of the exercises, and less than 4 out of 10 people shared the book with a friend. The group that actively used the book in this way had a much better outcome than those who didn't. Forty percent of those who actively worked with the book became abstinent from all symptoms compared to 5% of those whose compliance was poor.

We were intrigued by these findings. Beforehand, when there was a therapeutic failure we had a tendency to blame ourselves:

- Perhaps we didn't explain ourselves clearly enough?
- Perhaps we were too hard or too soft on our patients?
- Perhaps we didn't provide enough structure or too much, and so on?

Now we could clearly see that a major factor in the success of therapy was the clients' motivation to engage in treatment.

We therefore started to explore ways of increasing motivation. We became interested in the work of Prochaska and DiClemente (1986), two American psychologists who had addressed this issue in the context of various behaviours that raised health concerns (smoking, alcohol). These authors examined the processes by which people change behaviours. Their model fitted theoretically into the style of therapy (motivational interviewing) described by Miller and Rollnick (1991). Miller and Rollnick described how the behaviour of the therapist had a marked effect on compliance with treatment. A confrontational style led to resistance and non-compliance, whereas a supportive empathic response improved compliance. They therefore developed a therapeutic style of interaction which aimed to maximise the clients' motivation to change. This treatment method has been further refined in the field of addiction into motivational enhancement therapy (Miller, Zweben, DiClemente, & Rychtarik, 1992).

The Workbook, *Motivational Enhancement Therapy* (see Appendix, p.CG76), is an excellent supplement to self-care and can provide a framework for "guided self-care". It is aimed at providing the theoretical rationale and practical details of motivational enhancement therapy for bulimia nervosa.

THE THERAPEUTIC RELATIONSHIP

Clients with bulimia nervosa are often markedly ambivalent about treatment. Although they admit readily that their symptoms, particularly the bingeing, cause them distress, there is often reluctance to change, especially if they are asked to contemplate giving up their maladaptive weight control methods.

As a therapist you need to be warm and empathic. Indicate that you want a collaborative relationship. You will need to stress that you will give and want feedback in the sessions. Working with *Bit(e) by Bit(e)*, opens the way for choice. The client can take responsibility for decision-making.

The client with bulimia nervosa may seem open, vulnerable, engaging and charming, and an exciting prospect to work with. However, before you get seduced into complacency think about the interpersonal schemata that are common in these women. Often, these include polar opposites including the drive to please and rebelliousness, mistrust of others and childlike dependence, and putting people on a pedestal or denigrating them.

At the beginning of therapy, or even throughout the whole of therapy, the client may try to please you and bring back perfect diaries. If the diaries almost seem too good to be true it is worth saying something like: "I have frequently come across clients who try so hard to please the therapist, that they try not to upset them by bringing diaries which show that they haven't been eating regularly or that they have been bingeing frequently. I don't want our relationship to be like that. I will need you to give me accurate feedback on how you are doing. Also, I will want you to do this in the sessions we have together. I may say something that gets you irritated or sad and I hope you will be able to point out if I have stepped on a 'corn' or misunderstood you."

However, the client can quickly switch to another state either within or between sessions when she will become angry, rebellious and non-compliant. At times the client may present like a distraught child begging you to do something; however, in the next session they can appear contemptuous of the suggestions made to help. The therapist can feel exasperated when homework is not done or when the client sneers or complains about the therapeutic strategies. For example, they may bitterly carp on that keeping a food diary will only make their eating worse. They may fail to show up for sessions or phone with last minute excuses. It is all too easy to be cast in the role of a vengeful, persecuting bully. Stop if you feel yourself getting angry or starting to retaliate. Draw back from entering the field as a victimiser. Stop if your patience is being stretched beyond endurance by trying to accommodate erratic sessions or long, frequent phone consultations. There is no need for you to play the role of a resentful victim.

It is important to set the limits of your therapeutic relationship at the beginning. Come to an agreement on how your sessions will be spaced out. Explain to your clients how they can leave messages if a session needs to be cancelled. Let them know that it may take a few days before you can return a telephone call. Be clear about the rules. For example, if they fail to attend for a session without cancelling, then that session will be lost to them.

Understanding the transference and counter-transference is an important part of management. It is important to realise that resistance and denial result from the interpersonal relationship between you and your client and you can do something about it.

INTRODUCING *BIT(E) BY BIT(E)*

The way that you introduce *Bit(e) by Bit(e)* to your client and the way that you use it can be very important. Discuss your mutual expectations about the book. For example, you might want to say something like: "This book describes people who have similar experiences to you. It describes the skills that they have learnt and used to get over their problems. It also includes advice and information that others have found helpful. Many people find it helpful to read it as it stops them feeling all alone." You want to raise their curiosity about how others have coped but not to imply that there is only one way and that they must take your advice and do exactly what you and the book say. Leave an element of choice for the client.

Some of the advantages that they can get from using the book are that they can pace the rate of learning and can make an informed decision about whether or not they are ready for change. Also, the book will be on hand when difficulties arise. Prepare them to be realistic in their expectations about the course of their treatment. Often it is bumpy. They may do very well initially and be full of enthusiasm, but will be blown off course by the next crisis that they encounter. One way to get across this idea is to ask them to consider their eating disorder as an Achilles heel. It is their weak point in response to stress. This does not mean that they are defective in some way. Normalise the stress response for them. For example you can say: "People respond to stress in different ways, some secrete more acid in their stomachs and get ulcers, others may fur up their coronary arteries, yet others use alcohol." You can suggest that unlike people with other stress-related problems they at least have an external marker or sign that they are in difficulties and can do something about it, rather than suddenly collapsing with a heart attack. Thus, the book should always be kept at hand for them to deal with lapses and relapses and should be read at times when they feel that they are slipping.

It is then important to go over some practical details. How much reading will your client be able to do? Will there be difficulties in having time or a place to read the book? Can she set aside some time every day or on certain days of the week? Will she want or be able to show it to a friend or a member of the family? Also, you need to indicate that the book will be an integral part of the next session. Tell her that you will review the workbook exercises with her the following week. Ensure that in your sessions you will review all the homework, jottings and ideas that they have had over the week. It is important to familiarise yourself with the content of *Bit(e) by Bit(e)* so that you can tailor your assignments to the client you are working with. It is important to adjust the chapters and activities in the book to the stage of motivation of your client (see later).

THEORETICAL BACKGROUND ABOUT BEHAVIOUR CHANGE

An influential concept that has emerged from observations of the process of behaviour change is the transtheoretical model of Prochaska and DiClemente (1986). According to this model, behaviour change is conceptualised in two dimensions: the motivational aspect or "stages of change", and the activities brought into play to achieve the goal, so-called "processes" of change. These authors have defined five stages of change:

- precontemplation;
- contemplation;
- preparation/determination;
- action; and
- maintenance.

These represent various levels of motivation. Thus *precontemplators* are not interested in considering change and indeed fail to acknowledge that they have a behaviour which needs to be changed. At this stage, information rather than advice on action is appropriate. Parents may ring up in distress and crisis because they have noticed that their daughter is vomiting. Occasionally, these clients then get brought to the clinic by their families.

In the *contemplation* stage individuals are willing to examine the problems associated with their eating disorder and consider the implications of change, but are unlikely to take action. At this stage, they are more open to education. However, they need to resolve the ambivalence they have about wanting to change. This means identifying the negative aspects of their present behaviour and making sure that they are willing to give them up. This stage can lead into the *preparation / determination* stage in which there is readiness to change, a desire for help but often difficulty in knowing what to do.

In the *action* stage, the individual has made a commitment to change and may have begun to modify her behaviour. This is a time of great stress and there is a need for support and encouragement from professionals and from their social network. Relapse prevention techniques are useful once an individual is in the *maintenance* phase.

The actual process of change is not a simple linear progression as just described; instead, individuals oscillate between stages. Prochaska and

DiClemente (1992) use the model of a revolving door with some individuals going around several times before achieving their long-term goals.

FACILITATING CHANGE

Pitching Your Interventions at the Right Level

This model has implications for treatment, in that it is important to match your intervention to the client's stage of change. For example, it is no use offering a client with bulimia nervosa advice on how to eat regularly unless she has reached the action phase. A mismatch between the intervention promoted by the therapist and the stage of change of the client leads to resistance (Rollnick, Kinnersly, & Stott, 1993).

Motivational enhancement therapy addresses where the client is on the cycle of change and assists the person to move through the stages toward successful sustained change. For this approach the contemplation and determination phases are the most critical. The objective is to help clients address two basic issues:

- The first is how much of a problem their bulimia poses for them and how it is affecting them both positively and negatively. Tipping the balance of the pros and cons of bulimia towards change is essential for movement from contemplation to determination. In the contemplation phase, the client assesses the possibility of change and the costs/benefits of changing the problem behaviour. Clients consider whether they will be able to make a change and how that change will affect their lives.
- The second is that individuals who have made unsuccessful attempts in the past need encouragement to go through the cycle again. In the determination stage, clients develop a firm resolve to take action. This resolve is coloured by past experiences with attempts at change.

Understanding the cycle of change can help the therapist remain empathic rather than frustrated about the level of clients' motivation and it also provides a rationale to help them provide direction in their interventions.

Other Factors

Not only do we need to consider how motivated people are to change but how confident they feel in their ability to undertake the work that is necessary to bring about change. Clients who have very low self-esteem have difficulty thinking that they can do anything about the situation. If people have been brought up to have very little autonomy in their lives they may find it difficult to believe they have the skills and confidence to do anything about it. If people have clinical depression they may lack the judgement, motivation and skills to make progress.

ESSENTIALS OF MOTIVATIONAL INTERVIEWING

Several observations have suggested that therapists can and do influence motivation to change. Therapist expectancies for client change have been shown to influence client compliance and outcome. Therapists differ markedly in their "client retention rates". When clients are randomly assigned to therapists, their outcomes differ substantially depending on the therapist to whom they are assigned. By changing their therapeutic style between confrontational and client-centred approaches, therapists can drive client resistance both up and down. Client-resistance behaviour is in turn predictive of failure to change.

Simple actions such as a follow-up note or phone call by therapists can double the probability that clients will return for further treatment after an initial or missed session. Therapist empathy is associated with more favourable client outcomes. Therefore, motivation can be thought of not as a client attribute but as an interpersonal process between therapist and client. In conclusion, research clearly demonstrates that the interaction between therapist and client powerfully influences client resistance, compliance and change.

Miller and Sanchez (1994) reviewed many different forms of brief therapies and found that six components were common to them all and these could be subsumed under the acronym FRAMES.

F-Feedback Personal feedback regarding the client's individual status rather than blanket summaries.

R-Responsibility An emphasis on the individual's freedom of choice. "It's up to you: you're free to decide to change or not. You're the one who has to do it if it's going to happen."

A-Advice Clear recommendation or advice on the need to change in a supportive and concerned rather than authoritarian manner.

M-Menu A variety of options or solutions offered to the client.

E-Empathy An empathic, reflective, warm and supportive counselling style.

S-Self-efficacy A style that reinforces the expectation of change.

Also, most brief interventions include follow-up contacts which may reinforce change even if solely conducted for research.

In part, some of the lessons from this meta-analysis have been incorporated into motivational enhancement therapy. This in turn uses motivational interviewing as the form of therapist-client interaction. An outline of the essentials of motivational interviewing is shown in the following section.

GUIDELINES FOR MOTIVATIONAL INTERVIEWING

General Principles

1. The goal is to improve intrinsic motivation to change rather than impose change externally.
2. Develop a discrepancy between present behaviour and broader goals; between self-concept and behaviour.
3. Express empathy and acceptance by selective reflective listening.
4. Support self-efficacy, hope or optimism.
5. Improve self-esteem.
6. Readiness to change is a product of the therapist and client interaction.
7. The therapeutic relationship should be collaborative.

Do

1. Let the client present the arguments for change by articulating and resolving her ambivalence.
2. Start with the client's (not the therapist's) concerns.
3. Focus on eliciting the client's concerns.
4. Emphasise personal choice and responsibility for deciding future behaviour. Negotiate goals and strategies.
5. Explore and reflect the client's perceptions.
6. Use empathic reflection selectively with a spin towards change.
7. Reflect feelings, concerns and self-motivational statements.
8. Reflect with a statement starting with "you" as the subject.
9. Summarise periodically.
10. Make a short summary of sessions at the beginning and end of each session.
11. Offer advice and feedback where appropriate.
12. Use positive restructuring of the client's statements to improve self-esteem and self-efficacy.

Don't

1. Argue, lecture or persuade with logic.
2. Assume an authoritarian or expert role.
3. Give expert advice at the beginning.
4. Order, direct, warn or threaten.
5. Do most of the talking.
6. Get into debates or struggles over diagnostic labelling.
7. Make moral statements, criticise, preach or judge.

8. Ask questions to which the client gives short answers.
9. Respond to a client's response to an open-ended question with another question.
10. Ask a series of questions (three or more) in a row.
11. Tell the client that she has a problem.
12. Prescribe solutions or a certain course of action.
    (Adapted from P. Hayward personal communication.)

One of the principles of this approach is that head-to-head conflict is unhelpful. What is more helpful is a collaborative, shoulder-to-shoulder relationship in which you and the client tackle the problem together. The client's motivation to change can be enhanced by using a negotiation method in which the client, not the practitioner, articulates the benefits and costs involved. Education and confrontation can lead to resistance, whereas empathy and support can facilitate the behaviour change.

THE GOAL OF THE THERAPEUTIC ALLIANCE

One of the first steps is to establish where exactly your client is on the road to change. Does she understand what change might entail? Is she willing to accept some costs? For example, a client with a strong genetic predisposition to obesity who maintains her weight in the normal range only by tightly restricting her diet and vomiting, may be prepared to sacrifice her health to prevent herself becoming obese. She will be reluctant to give up the methods of weight control she has discovered.

Your job is to try to gently lead your client along the pathway of change. As a guide or teacher it is useful to remember a philosophical point noted by Pascal and observed by educationalists since this time, "people are generally better persuaded by reasons they have discovered themselves than by those given by others". Your task as a therapist is therefore to act as a facilitator to help the sufferer discover for herself the reasons why she might want to change and perhaps, just as importantly, the reasons why she may not want to change.

Progress can only take place when you have helped your client resolve this ambivalence. This is the subject of chapter 1 of *Getting Better Bit(e) by Bit(e)*, which is called "The Way Forward".

A motivational enhancement therapy approach has the assumption that the responsibility and capability for change lie within the client. Your job as a therapist is to mobilise the client's inner resources as well as those available within the client's natural helping relationships.

As a therapist you need to use the five basic motivational principles as defined by Miller and Rollnick (1991):

1. Express empathy
2. Develop discrepancy

3. Avoid argumentation
4. Roll with resistance
5. Support self-efficacy

1. *Express Empathy*

The relationship with the client should communicate respect. Although at times you will need to act as a knowledgeable consultant for the most part you will need to be a supportive companion. The emphasis is on the client's decision to change or not, although you should provide a subtle undertow in the direction of change. Reflective listening underpins this component of therapy.

2. *Develop Discrepancy*

The drive to change can be fuelled when the client recognises a discrepancy between where she is and where she wants to be (i.e. *vis-à-vis* her personal goals and aspirations). Motivational enhancement therapy aims to enhance and focus the client's attention on to such discrepancies. You probably will need to develop a discrepancy by helping the client to become aware of the consequences of her abnormal eating pattern.

3. *Avoid Argumentation*

Handled poorly, ambivalence and discrepancy lead to defensive coping strategies such as stubborn negativism. So, having friends and family who critically point out to a sufferer what she is doing to herself may not be helpful. Your job and skills should be to let the client voice the adverse effects of bulimia and to devalue the positive effects.

4. *Roll with Resistance*

Resistance will emerge time and time again. Don't try to fight it down, rather try to explore in more detail the underlying ambivalence by reflective listening.

5. *Support Self-efficacy*

Try to foster an environment that nurtures optimism so that change can occur. Emphasise environmental or prognostic factors that engender hope. If you do not provide this a discrepancy crisis will lead to defensive coping (rationalisation or denial). This is a natural and understandable protective process. If one has little hope that things can change, there is little reason to face the problem.

Reflective Listening

This is an essential skill in motivational interviewing. It is the foundation upon which all other skills are built and is a safe fall-back whenever you are stuck. When done well it looks deceptively easy but it is a demanding skill. It involves having a hypothesis-testing approach to listening. A good listening response tests your hypothesis. However, the best type of reflective listening response is a statement although this may seem presumptuous and strange at first. The best word to help you get started with reflection is "you". For example, use the following stems at first:

- So you feel...
- It sounds like you...
- You're wondering if...
- You....

However, motivational interviewing differs from client-centred counselling in that you are trying to put a spin on your reflections so as to point your clients into the direction of change. You want to help them discover the negative aspects of their behaviour and come up with self-motivating statements. You want to help them explore the positive reinforcers and to see whether they might be able to think of alternative ways of getting the same effect.

THE FIRST MEETING

There are two phases to treatment: building motivation for change and strengthening commitment to change. Even if your client appears to be committed to change it is worthwhile going through all the initial stages so that you can see the strength of the motivation and consolidate the commitment.

This phase is to tip the motivational balance in favour of perceived benefits of changing eating patterns. One of the major strategies is to elicit self-motivating statements.

Self-motivating Statements

Motivational psychology has found that if people are enticed to speak and act in a new way their beliefs and values shift in the direction. Thus, one of the first steps to get change is to foster an environment in which the client will be able to articulate her desire to change. This has some grounding in self-perception theory, which suggests that people learn what they believe by hearing themselves talk (Bem, 1967).

It may be helpful to start the interview by using some of the following questions to get the client to define her problem. However, it is not a good idea to just have a battery of questions which you fire at your client like a machine gun. Reflective listening is important after each question. This will help the client know that she is understood. Therefore, after the answer in each domain either repeat, paraphrase or summarise her response. Whenever possible try to capture the emotional tone as well. Avoid, whenever possible, asking more than three questions in a row.

1. Problem Recognition

- What do you think is your problem?
- Are other people worried about you?
- What are they worried about?

2. Concerns

The following are the stem questions that can be helpful in structuring the beginning of your interview:

It helps me if I can break up your concerns into small areas.
- In what way has your eating disorder affected your physical health?
- In what way has your eating disorder affected your psychological health?
- In what way has your eating disorder affected your family life?
- In what way has your eating disorder affected your social life?
- In what way has your eating disorder affected your romantic life?
- In what way has your eating disorder affected your education and career?
- In what way has you eating disorder affected your financial security?
- Some people find that their eating disorder gets them into trouble with the law. Has that happened to you?

Here is an example of an extract of dialogue:

Therapist: Do you have any concerns about how your physical health may have been affected by your eating disorder?
Client: Well, there is the problem about my teeth.
Therapist: You are concerned about them. (STATEMENT)
Client: Well yes, I am aware that I have had problems for several years, they have been very sensitive to cold drinks. Over the last few months I have had two or three fillings drop out. I have been to the dentist and I have two to three hundred pounds' worth of work that needs doing.
Therapist: Your teeth have suffered the effects of your eating disorder. (STATEMENT) What do you think will happen if you don't make a change?

If there are difficulties in eliciting clients' concerns you may find it helpful to be the devil's advocate and take the voice of your client's resistance.

Therapist: Can I tell you one concern I have? This treatment requires a fair amount of motivation from people and frankly I'm not sure from what you have told me that you are motivated enough to go through with it. Do you think we should go ahead now or wait a little until you have had time to reflect more about it?

Listening with Empathy: Reflective Listening

The foregoing details how you can encourage your client to start talking, but how you respond to her is of great importance. The therapeutic skill of accurate empathy (Rogers, 1957) is of great importance. The therapist listens carefully to what the client is saying and then reflects it back, often in a modified or reframed form with some acknowledgement of the client's expressed or implicit emotion.

This skill of reflective listening has many advantages. It gives the client feedback that she has been listened to and understood. This technique can build up empathy and lead the client to feel supported. This builds up a good working alliance. This method also acts to clarify what the client has said and so can reinforce ideas put forward by the client. The key element of motivational interviewing is to put a spin on the reflection by using it selectively. You can reinforce certain statements and ignore others. You will obviously want to highlight the statements that tip the balance towards change. Thus, clients will not only hear themselves articulate a self-motivating statement, but also, they will hear you saying that they said it and perhaps also see it written down in a feedback letter. If the client is very ambivalent you need to address this with a double-sided reflection acknowledging the other side of the balance. If possible use the word "and" to join the two statements rather than "but". Here are some double-sided reflections:

- Your bulimia gives you a sense of being in control and at the same time you recognise that you are getting further into debt.

- It is confusing, you are aware of the dangers to your health arising from your bulimia and you worry what would happen to your weight if you gave it up.

Reflective listening in this manner is not easy. Perhaps the use of the word "reflective" is poor as it implies that you are being a blank mirror processing nothing. Rather, you are being a filter trying to only let the self-motivating statements through to be reflected back. This means that you are having to think twice as fast as the client. You will be very busy hearing what she says and analysing whether it could be self-motivating or not. Also, try to understand the emotional tone behind it from both her verbal and non-verbal communication. You will be slow in your responses until you are used to it. Don't be afraid of leaving pauses while you think. These can be helpful even when you have developed expertise, as they are an important signal that you are thinking. It is much better to be ponderous and quiet rather than to participate in a ping-pong conversational game.

Feedback within sessions is used to reflect and highlight problems and concerns which the client puts forward. Thus, during the assessment procedure it is helpful to summarise the problems. This can be done after each domain is mentioned, again after all the difficulties have been elicited and finally at the end of the interview.

- So to summarise, you have been concerned about your health. You have noticed that you become tired more easily. You have become more irritable with your family. You don't find pleasure in going out with friends like you used to and it has been more difficult concentrating on your studies.

The tone of the interview can get very low and negative and it may be helpful to interject some affirmatory statements. This is particularly important for those with low self-esteem.

- In the face of all these problems it is impressive that you were able to judge that you were somewhat overwhelmed and have chosen to come here to get help.

It may be useful to make an assessment of the client's self-efficacy using questions such as:

- What makes you think if you decide to change you could do it?
- What do you think would work for you if you decided to change?
- Have there been times in the past when you were able to control your chaotic eating?

Orienting Yourself

One of the first tasks, once you have made an alliance to work together, is to establish where your client is on her pathway to change. Ask her to fill in her first worksheet from the Workbook (Appendix, p.CG77).

Once your client has done this, it is useful to use it as a starting point in your negotiation of change. Here are some questions that might be of use:

- It is interesting that you have given yourself x. Why have you given yourself that rather than 1 or 10?
- What would have to happen for you to move from x to 10?
- What would you need from me to help you move from x to 10?
- Have you ever been at 1? What helped you to move from 1 to x?
- What would you need from your family to help you move from x to 10?

It may be useful to give this simple pen and paper task at regular intervals during therapy and to plot the changes in these over time.

WRITTEN FEEDBACK

In addition to verbal feedback throughout the session, a letter to the client gives the opportunity for more structured feedback. In our practice this has replaced the usual letter to the referral agency. (The latter is now a short note outlining plans for management.) Written feedback has the advantage that it can be referred to later by the client and also shown to others in her network. Furthermore, this demonstrates that you have listened and are willing to be actively helpful.

The letter should contain statements to increase motivation which have been culled from the assessment interview. It may be useful to acknowledge in the letter that it is merely a first attempt to get understanding and it may need to be changed later in the light of joint work.

Example of a Feedback Letter Following the First Meeting

Helen had had 25 years of eating difficulties and although this had restricted her life she had adapted to this. She had had several attempts at treatment before coming to us. She decided to come for help because her stepdaughter had developed an eating problem. In the feedback letter it was important to document how the bulimia had affected her life and yet how ambivalent she felt about the need for treatment.

Dear Helen,
   You came to see me with a problem with your eating.
   It is difficult for you to be certain how much of a problem this is and how much it concerns you. (Ambivalence)
   You tightly restrict your diet but this then leads to binges. Your preoccupation with weight and shape drives you to exercise

relentlessly in the face of injury. For example, you take pain killers and run despite the stress fracture in your foot. (Problem recognition)

This preoccupation with weight and shape has overshadowed your whole adult life. You often feel tense, guilty and low in your mood. This has affected your relationship with your partner, in that he finds you moody and that you cannot be completely open with him. At the present time you feel guilty in that you think that your eating disorder may have influenced your stepdaughter. You are concerned that you have been a poor role model for her. Your work has suffered as often you do not have the confidence to go out to chase for assignments. (Concerns)

At the age of 21 you developed anorexia, your weight fell from 9 stones to 5½ stones with amenorrhoea for a year. Over the last 27 years your weight has fluctuated between 8½ and 10½ stones. You have resorted to the use of slimming tablets when they have been available to you. Your work performance and social life are impaired as when you feel "too fat" you cancel and avoid outside activities. At times you have felt so low that you have contemplated suicide. (History of the problem)

In childhood you always felt ostracised and different to your peers. You felt very much an outsider as a "scholarship" girl with parents in a different social class to everyone else around you. At law school you remained separate in that you began a relationship with a lecturer. Within this relationship you were both physically and mentally abused. Your confidence was severely undermined by this and you felt totally powerless. It is possible that your eating symptoms developed as a means of coping with your outrage and violation. Although outwardly successful you remain uncertain of your talents. (Possible antecedents and function of eating disorder)

You obviously have great difficulty in deciding how much help you might need and want. Other things have often taken priority in your life. Only you can decide whether you want to change or not. (Level of motivation)

I look forward to seeing you next week.

Best wishes,

It is important later to go through this feedback letter, with the client, to check it for accuracy and impact. Ask how it made her feel reading it. What bits didn't seem right? Was she concerned or puzzled by any of it? At the same time you may be able to give feedback from any investigations that have been undertaken, the blood test results, etc.

Bolster Self-efficacy

You may want to lighten the tone of negativity that might arise by giving some affirming statements such as praising the client for recognising her difficulty and coming for help. Try to positively connote statements made by her or given by others. If possible, try to reframe the problem. One way to do this is to describe bulimia as a stress response. As such it is a signal that things are not all right. The advantage of this way of reacting to stress is that it is obvious and a clear signal. In some people, stress leads to stomach ulcers or heart attacks, or even other problems such as cancer. They may not have any prior warning of difficulties. In contrast, reacting to stress with bulimia gives them a chance to work on their problems. Bulimia is a response to stress in young people. Stress is a fact of life so that if they can find better ways of responding to the stress then they will have the advantage over others in learning adaptive skills early on.

SESSIONS 1–3

The next stage in treatment is to use the Workbook, *Motivational Enhancement Therapy* (see Appendix, p.CG76), and *Getting Better Bit(e) by Bit(e)* for the first 1 to 3 sessions, in preparation for the action phase. The length of time spent at this stage and the number of exercises completed depends on the readiness to change ascertained on Worksheet 1 (*To Change Or Not To Change?*, Appendix, p.CG77) .

Chapter 1 in *Bit(e) by Bit(e)* contains some exercises that can be used as the basis for a motivational approach. This chapter starts with a self-report scale (Table 1.1) that measures bulimic behaviour. The aim of this is to highlight the extent of the symptomatic difficulties. This scale has also been used as an outcome measure for bulimic behaviour and you may find it useful to monitor change over treatment and at follow-up.

Some education and information about the consequences of weight control and dieting is useful in order to apply the motivational exercises effectively. In *Bit(e) by Bit(e)* we encourage clients to read chapters 2–6 before starting any active work. You may be able to facilitate this by encouraging your client to make notes to ask you about anything she didn't understand, or which seemed very relevant to her or which she wants more information about.

It is important when giving feedback about medical risks that you do not adopt a confrontational attitude as this will increase resistance. Offer the client choices about whether she wants you to give her more information—is there a resource available, videos, etc. that she can tap for further details?

Defining the Ambivalence

One of the most important features of motivational enhancement therapy is to clearly define the ambivalence. You may need to spend some time doing this. Often, there is such shame and disgust about bulimic behaviours that the clients find it difficult to acknowledge the positive benefits it gives them. We therefore often find it useful spending several sessions trying to define this vacillation.

There are several ways of highlighting the ambivalence. You can ask about the good things and the not so good things about dieting or vomiting. Another way is to address your client as if they had two parts, a bulimic part and a normal part that wants to get well. We have visually depicted the bulimic, weight-controlling part as a boa constrictor (see Worksheet 2: *Is Change Reasonable?*, Appendix, p.CG78). This means that as a therapist you can join with the part that wants to get well and together with the client tackle the bulimic part. This stops you having to nag and battle with the client. The exercise focuses on the current difficulties clients have with their bulimia and, it is hoped, will lead them to generate self-motivating thoughts.

We have used a more formal method in chapter 1 of *Bit(e) by Bit(e)* "First Steps" (p.4). Here, we illustrate the use of a decisional balance sheet. This can be useful to make the factors that lead to ambivalence about change explicit.

There is a strong association between the stage of change and the decisional balance sheet. In bulimia nervosa, the factors that are often placed on the "reasons to keep bulimia" side are weight and shape issues, and the need to use bulimia to vent emotional distress. Before change can occur it will be necessary to focus on these issues.

The main positive reinforcers for bulimic behaviour may be to ensure that weight remains in the normal range. Further understanding about the control of body weight may be gained by the client reading chapter 7, "Jack Spratt's Wife" (p.59).

The other common reinforcer for bulimic behaviour is the relief of distressing moods. If this is the case you might suggest that the client reads *Mind over Mood* (Greenberger & Padesky, 1995) and the companion volume *Clinician's Guide to Mind Over Mood* (Padesky & Greenberger, 1995). This is a self-treatment book that teaches cognitive behavioural strategies for emotional distress. Or you may want to teach the distress tolerance skills outlined in Linehan (1983a,b).

We have found that it is often illuminating to ask your client to write letters to the bulimia nervosa as if it were a friend and as if it were an enemy. This promotes more emotional expression and comes from the heart rather than the head.

Here are examples of letters produced by a client of ours.

Letter to Bulimia Nervosa: The Enemy

Dear Bulimia,

My lifelong enemy. I won't start by asking how you are because I know you always survive—I can always count on you being in my life lurking about somewhere in the background or sometimes in the forefront of my life. Whether I am conscious of you or not you'll always pull through showing your ugly head, drawing me towards you, leaving my confidence and self-control.

You hang over my life like a black cloud which is about to burst, so much rain will pour out and I'll end up feeling wet, cold and alone.

I used to be very religious but you made me forget my beliefs, as I deceived and thieved from my parents. I have lost most of my friends due to you as I never wanted to socialise at school or after school. I feel that I have disappointed my family. I was clever, obtaining very good grades at GCSE, but you made me lose my concentration when studying for my A levels. I was always too busy thinking about my next meal rather than physics, chemistry or biology. I would cook meals which would have fed a whole family as a break in between studying. I was so busy bingeing and purging that I failed my A levels and consequently didn't get a university place.

You boosted my looks but not my self-esteem or self-confidence. You made me feel guilty about the food I eat and the way I behave in removing it. I feel ashamed of my actions and you have made me have a feeling of no control over these actions.

You have made my relationship with other members of the family very strained. I am always arguing with my sisters or parents for no reason. You have changed my emotions and my personality as I have mood swings from "normal" to sometimes quite a depressive nature (because of you I tried to commit suicide to remove you and me).

You are slowly decaying my teeth and in the future you may also be responsible for other health problems and for me not being able to have children. Most importantly, because of you I am a worry to the people I care about the most, especially my fiancé. He cannot trust me fully because of the actions you make me do. If you were not a part of my life he would not have to worry unnecessarily about my health. He would not have to be wary about whether what I eat will remain after it has been consumed. Life would run more smoothly with one less thing to worry about.

Why can't you let go of me and allow me to get on with my life—whatever that may mean. What I'm really saying is that life's hard enough without having to cope with the pressure which you put me under. Leave me now, I've had you on my back for long enough. There's one last thing left to say, I'll get you right out of my life one day, I don't know when but I'll certainly know when you've gone—and to be sure you won't return I'll close the door to my mind so tightly you'll never be able to come through again.

It is clear that this letter has many self-motivating statements in it. The client clearly documents the ways in which the bulimia nervosa has harmed her in every facet of her life.

Letter to Bulimia Nervosa: The Friend

Dear Bulimia,

Thank you for always being there. You are with me day and night, wherever I may be, whatever I may be doing. You are like my shadow, my best friend. You know everything about me—you are a part of me. No one has ever been so close to me.

I talk to you and, although you cannot speak to me, I get comfort from confiding in you. I know that you listen and understand.

Whatever happens, whatever events or changes life brings, you will always remain the same. You will always be there and never change.

You make me feel special by making me different. You give me something that none of my friends or family have.

Your presence is a comfort to me. I think the greatest comfort is knowing that, even when I'm on my own, I'm not alone.

You have taught me so many habits and tricks which I have become good at. It is an achievement and I get satisfaction from knowing that I'm good at what I do and that no one else can do it.

I have a slim figure now and I look good to other people. Before, people would ridicule the way I looked but with your help instead of being ignored I am noticed. I can wear the latest fashions without looking like a stuffed turkey (bursting at the seams!). I also don't have to watch the calories that I consume as I know by having you as my friend I will never become fat. With the help of you I have been able to reach the ideal weight and size that I want.

This letter illustrates the way that bulimia nervosa enables the client to fulfil her somewhat grandiose desire to be admired and to be the perfect size. The bulimia also plays the part of a confidante.

Working with the Letters

Once your client has written the letters ask her to read them out for you. How did it make her feel writing it? Perhaps you can feed back to your client how it made you feel. (Often, clients with eating disorders have a great deal of difficulty labelling their emotions. They may have a limited vocabulary with which to do this so that hearing you labelling emotions can be very helpful.) Reflect back to them the issues that they have highlighted as important. Reflect back on the content of letters, summarise if possible. Here is an example of a double-sided reflection:

- In your letter to the enemy you seem to be angry and frightened and sad that Bulimia Nervosa has destroyed many of your core values, academic proficiency, moral attitude, religious beliefs, and family relationships. On the other hand, it has improved your looks and been like a companion. It is as if you feel you have sold your soul to the devil.

Is there any difference in the length of the two letters? Do the same points feature in both letters? This is a reflection of the underlying confusion that bulimic clients experience. Acknowledge each point that they make in the letter and ask them to expand on it. The common themes that are regarded as positive about bulimia nervosa are security, attractiveness and confidence. It may be helpful to suggest that these are issues that you will want to work on further.

Are there any other ways that they could get these positive effects which would be less self-destructive? How important are these positive effects to them? How convinced are they that bulimia nervosa is a friend/enemy after reading that letter? Ask them to mark it on a scale of 0–100%. If possible include affirmatory statements. Praise the work involved in thinking about the possibilities of change.

DIFFICULTIES WITH CHANGE

Worksheet 3 (*Difficulties of Change,* Appendix, p.CG79) is used to focus on the idea of change and what would be involved. It shows a victim trying to remove herself from the snake. The aim is to encourage a focus on the difficulties of change and recovery and the ambivalence about the ability to pass through these phases.

Apart from writing notes about how your client will be affected by change under the headings: health (physical and psychological), social life, family life, and career, encourage her to write letters or poems or draw pictures to illustrate the difficulties of change. How will she cope if her weight does increase? If she becomes more irritable and lacks confidence now what could she do about it?

Feed back and summarise her concerns. Whenever possible, emphasise and affirm the strength of her self-motivation statements. Liberal use of affirmation can prevent your client from getting cold feet when thinking about difficulties of change. Several strategies can be helpful. You may want to convey alternative attributions (reframe), normalise ambivalence, recognise the barriers and yet support continued exploration of the problems and provide positive reinforcement.

For example, a double-sided reflection can be a useful form of feedback:

- You have clearly defined the difficulties of change and you have clearly articulated the very good reasons you have for wanting to change.

Reframing the problem can be an important step in looking at it in a different manner. It may be possible to communicate that the problem is solvable and changeable. For example, many women with bulimia nervosa lead very isolated lives, doing jobs that they hate and their one pleasure is to binge eat at night. This can be reframed as:

- You may need to find alternative rewards to give yourself in the evening for successfully handling a difficult day.

Others either don't have the skills or are wary of sharing their difficulties with others:

- You don't want to appear selfish by imposing additional stress on your friends and family by opening up to them about your difficulty.
- You absorb all the stress and tension and put on a bright face.

Yet others use bulimia as a way of tolerating a difficult relationship:

- Your bulimia is a way of avoiding conflict and disagreement in your marriage. Your bulimia helps preserve the status quo. Both you and your partner appear happy about this.

Once you have reached this level you will have probably discovered other behaviours/difficulties that need to be changed, for example, a barren lifestyle or a relationship difficulty. You will need to go back to Worksheet 1 to explore these in more detail to consider change. It is rather like some board game such as Monopoly when you keep reaching "Go". However, like the board game, you gradually accumulate more with each circuit.

CORE VALUES: GOAL-SETTING

Miller suggests that a potent way of promoting change is to highlight the dissonance between a person's current way of life and his or her core values (Miller & C'deBaca, 1994).

It therefore can be helpful to define your clients' core values. Ask them to reflect back on themselves before their eating disorder began.

- What were their hopes and aspirations then?
- Has their eating disorder prevented them from reaching their targets?

Worksheet 4 (*Future Times*, Appendix, p.CG80) aims to focus on thinking about the future. It shows the boa constrictor being put inside its pot.

In chapter 1, "The Way Forward" of *Bit(e) by Bit(e)* we tackle this issue by asking the reader to write letters in which they imagine the future with and without bulimia nervosa.

The aim of the letter to the future without bulimia nervosa is to promote the idea that there may be an alternative lifestyle possible without the eating disorder. It is particularly difficult for clients who have developed the illness early in their lives, and who have had the illness for a long time, to imagine life without bulimia.

Once your client has defined what their goals in life are, you may need to mark out the series of steps to be tackled on the way to achieving at least some of those goals. Aim to have some targets that are attainable reasonably quickly. There may be overt or covert road blocks to achieving these aims. A problem-solving, solution-focused, approach will be useful to work on these issues. However, remember before you dash into problem-solving mode it may be necessary to spend some time with reflective listening so that you have aired any ambivalence and difficulties they may have.

A step by step, problem-solving approach can be helpful. In summary this is to:

1. Define a personal goal.
2. Check this for congruence with other goals and values (i.e. for personal meaning).
3. Evaluate the situation and predict one's capacity to affect it and the likely consequences of achieving the aim.
4. Consider the range of processes available for achieving the goal. Ensure that a wide variety of options have been generated. Select the best in terms of likelihood of success and implementation, personal and social effects, short- and long-term effects.

5. Act.
6. Evaluate (a) the effectiveness of the action, how well did it meet the goals? (b) the consequences of the action in terms of predictions made about the effect on self and others (c) overall satisfaction.
7. Confirm or revise (a) the procedure (b) the aim.

Examples of this approach are given in Chapter 2 of *Bit(e) by Bit(e)*, "Tools for the Journey" p.13).

The letter to the future with the eating disorder still there is another method of further encouraging the expression of feelings and negative aspects about the eating disorder. Acknowledge any worries that emerge. This may be an opportunity to give feedback about the long-term effects of the illness. You may be able to empathise with your client's worries: "Yes it is tragic when we see someone aged 43 who wants to recover but who realises even if she does that her options in life are limited."

Miller has developed a strategy for working on this further by encouraging the client to rank her core values by sorting a set of cards that have values on them. These become a focus for further exploration.

It is hoped that after doing these exercises, the client will have made an emotional and cognitive reappraisal of the eating disorder and will have reached the preparation/determination stage.

Ask your client to fill in Worksheet 1 (*To Change or Not to Change?*, Appendix, p.CG77). Is there any change? If there is you can go on to the action phase.

MOVING INTO ACTION

Once you have successfully worked through the ambivalence you are ready to move into the action phase. This requires a focus on the skills and strategies that are illustrated in chapters 3–6 of *Bit(e) by Bit(e)*. Remember, there is no wrong or right way about any aspect of the treatment. Ambivalence will come and go. You will need to go back to a more motivational position from time to time. Don't forget the use of reflective listening. Miller states that giving someone five minutes of reflective listening is a great gift. Someone else has called it "verbal massage".

Timing is quite critical here and you need to know when someone is ready for action. Having the self-treatment book can take some of the risk out of trying to assess when this stage is reached, as the client can choose herself whether or not to take up some of the strategies and steps needed to change.

Clients Who Pose Problems in Gaining Motivation

It may be much more difficult to get clients who have underlying personality difficulties to move into the action phase. For example, clients with a borderline personality organisation will have rapidly changing and intense emotional reactions. They may use bulimia nervosa as a vent for their intense emotions and be reluctant to give up this release mechanism. Those with avoidant personalities are more reluctant to give up bulimia nervosa, their friend. Such clients will need help in order to understand their underlying interpersonal schemata. These clients will probably need a more intense type of treatment such as Ryle's cognitive analytical therapy (Ryle, 1990), or Young's schema-focused work (Young, 1992), or Linehan's dialectical therapy (Linehan, 1993a,b). Clients with these sorts of difficulties are probably best referred to a specialised unit.

Another group of clients who are less motivated to change are those with a strong genetic predisposition to obesity. These clients will have difficulty maintaining their weight within the normal range and will be extremely reluctant to give up their weight-control practices. This is not an easy problem to tackle. Treatments for obesity are largely ineffective and yet there is intense sociocultural stigma against obesity.

It is important to set realistic goals with these clients (they should probably not aim to hold their body weight in the lower half of the normal range). They will need extra strategies to replace the bulimic weight-controlling strategies such as incorporating exercise into their lifestyle or cutting down on fat-containing food. Group approaches may help such clients as the support of people with the same problem may help counterbalance the stigma of society.

Clients who are markedly depressed or who have high levels of symptoms may be unable to participate actively in treatment as their concentration, judgement and self-efficacy are impaired. In such cases it may be helpful to add an antidepressant, such as fluoxetine, as this may lift the depression and produce symptomatic relief from bingeing and vomiting.

Resistance

Do not think that just because you have worked with the ambivalence in the first few sessions that it will disappear. Expect to get resistance re-emerging. Remember, however, that resistance is not a one-sided attribute but arises from your relationship. It is a signal to you to change tack and perhaps to back down. You don't want to provoke your client into making stronger and stronger anti-motivational statements. Do not try to meet the resistance head on.

One technique of handling resistance is to give simple reflection or reflection with a degree of amplification. Beware of too much amplification because it can backfire. Double-sided reflection can be helpful. Also, you may need to go with the resistance and acknowledge that change may be asking too much and that the client has the right to choose what to do.

COMMITMENT TO CHANGE

Ask your client to fill in Worksheet 5 (*Plans for Change*, Appendix, p.CG81). This is an opportunity to feed back on all the sessions done so far.

Summary Letter

It is useful for you to summarise the progress the client has made. Do this verbally but it is also a good idea to write a letter outlining the content of the sessions and of the worksheets. Detail the ambivalence about change, the way in which the abnormal eating behaviour interferes with change and any plans that have been made to help with change.

Once you have managed to reach this stage it is useful to have a session with a significant support person. You will need to prepare the ground first and examine who is the most appropriate person to invite. Ask your client to fill in the support questionnaire given in Table 1.2 in chapter 1 of *Bit(e) by Bit(e)* for one or several people who she might think of as appropriate. Once she has chosen someone, invite him or her to a joint session with you. Might this person act as a cotherapist?

Usually, clients with bulimia nervosa have never told anyone else about their problem and so this can be an important first step. They can be gradually encouraged to be more open and to accept help and support from their helper. Remember that difficulties that arise with their helper may be mirroring difficulties in your therapeutic relationship which need to be resolved.

We found that only a quarter of our clients had taken up the suggestion, written in the book, of recruiting a friend or relative to help them with the task of overcoming their eating disorder. Intimate trusting relationships are a major problem area in bulimia nervosa. We invite all new clients to bring a friend or relative along for their first appointment at the eating disorder clinic. Whereas the majority of clients with anorexia nervosa bring a friend or family member, those with bulimia nervosa usually come alone.

Three-quarters of bulimic clients attending our clinic had experienced adversity in childhood with poor quality of their early relationships. Experiences of abuse, neglect and dislike may lead to a problematic attachment style which can persist into adulthood making it difficult to form and maintain secure and lasting relationships. It is interesting that a model of treatment of bulimia nervosa that focuses on relationships with others (interpersonal therapy) is as effective in the long term as a model of treatment with a focus on distorted attitudes to shape and weight (Fairburn et al., 1995).

In this brief form of treatment it is impossible to touch on all the important interpersonal issues, especially if these are longstanding and relate to personality difficulties. Therefore, we would recommend that in these more complex cases alternative forms of therapy should be given in a specialised unit. (We briefly touch on some interpersonal issues on p.CG41.)

In the session with the support person you may want to begin by asking your client to recapitulate on the work that you have done together and to introduce the support figure to the stage at which you are working. Aim to motivate the support person to contribute to the change process and elicit statements that will encourage your client to change. Ensure that the session does not degenerate into a mire of criticism or complaints. Negative feedback of this type leads to resistance rather than reform. Reframe any negative effects as a normal consequence of an eating disorder rather than moral failing. Try to keep the tone positive. You can do this by asking questions that will draw out positive comments:

- What are the positive signs you have noticed that make you think that X is ready for change?
- What are the things which give you hope that things will change for the better?

If the tone of the interaction is high in expressed emotion, criticism or hostility with little warmth, do your best to defuse the situation with reflective listening and reframing but if all this fails make do with sidelining the helper.

Keep the focus on your client's responsibility for change but explore tentatively how the supporter can give help.

SESSIONS 4–8: ACTION

Education and Advice: Practical Details about Food and Weight

Once you have successfully worked with the client and struggled with her ambivalence, motivation and lack of confidence about change, you are ready to enter the action stage. This is not to say that it is all plain sailing from now on. There will be times when you need to use the motivational strategies again to get around road blocks which will cross your path. It is helpful if you can work collaboratively with the client.

Ask her if there is any advice she needs and what treatment options she might want to think about. One advantage of working with *Bit(e) by Bit(e)* is that several change strategies are illustrated and you can let the client choose.

Your goal is to get your client to form a plan as to what to do about eating. Ensure that the plan is the client's, not yours: "Only you can change your eating and it's up to you." Ask the supporter " How do you think you might help?" All the time stress the theme that this is her responsibility and choice. That is not to say that you should not give advice when specific questions are asked. However, it is useful to follow it up with statements such as "Does that make sense to you? What do you think about it?"

Chapters 3–7 in *Bit(e) by Bit(e)* focus on the educational, behavioural and cognitive strategies that are necessary to control the abnormal eating behaviour. Encourage your client to read these and to discuss how relevant they would be to her.

Tasks and Skills

A good introduction to this part of the programme is to discuss with your client the pros and cons of dieting. This is not easy because the whole of our culture, fashion, media and health experts endorse dieting. The key tasks are to develop a regular meal pattern and to widen the range of foods eaten. Also introduce the concept of an "ABC" diary. This is described in chapter 2, "Tools for the Journey" in *Bit(e) by Bit(e)*.

Go through Worksheet 6 (*What Should I Weigh?*, Appendix, p.CG82) with the client to consider which weight range is reasonable.Then go through the calculations on Worksheet 7 (*What Do I Need to Eat?*, Appendix, p.CG83) to work out how many calories she should be aiming for. It often comes as quite a surprise to women to hear how much they can eat as part of a normal diet.

Ask your client to explain in her own words and her own experience the physiological homeostatic mechanisms that perpetuate bulimia nervosa. Has she grasped the concept of a series of self-perpetuating loops? Perhaps you could get her to sketch out with a diagram what she has understood from the chapters.

Ask the client, after she has read the book:

- Were there any people in it she identified with?
- Were any methods for change that were used by these people ones that she could use?
- Is she able to think of any other or better ways that might be suitable for her?

Be generous with affirmation to help raise confidence at surmounting the client's own difficulties that get in the way of change:

- You'd have to be pretty resourceful (inventive, clever, creative, imaginative) … to find an alternative solution to overeating when you are alone at night after the stresses and strains of the day.

Many clients find keeping a diary difficult and it is important not to get into a deadlock about it, with you saying "you must" and her passively or openly saying "I won't". Don't get polarised into thinking that there is only one right and wrong way of doing things. Think about alternative options.

Underlying Difficulties

The ABC diary can be a focus not only for monitoring and providing a structure for eating, but it can also be a template for understanding situations, thoughts and moods. The diary also monitors weekly activity. It is helpful to assess the relationship between activity/behaviour and mood. This may lead to interventions that restructure activities to improve coping with the precipitant of eating disorder behaviours. It may be helpful to draw up action plans with your client that specify alternative coping strategies to bingeing, purging and starvation. You may need to take an active part in problem-solving, to model the generation of ideas, with brainstorming.

Often, clients with eating disorders have difficulty clarifying, differentiating and rating emotions and so are not able to track moods easily with their diary. You may be able to help with this by reflective listening. More detailed practice may be necessary and you may want to ask the client to use the excellent book *Mind Over Mood* (Greenberger & Padesky, 1995). Once emotional states have been identified, the next stage is to identify and list automatic thoughts and then to modify the deeper assumptions and core beliefs.

Shifting Attitudes to Weight and Shape

Trying to shift the cognitive distortions about shape and weight in our current culture is an uphill struggle as they are ubiquitous. Worksheet 8 (*Stuck in the Dieting Pit*, Appendix, p.CG84) may be helpful. One way to tackle this issue is to try to moderate the maladaptive thoughts.

Look for an exaggerated statement your client makes about her weight or shape. (It need not be entirely false.) Bear in mind that often what she has *not* said is actually the most exaggerated part of the statement. If you can't find any statement, PROMPT her. Use cues, such as eating, in a session. List thoughts, before, during and after.

The following is an example of such a dialogue between therapist and client:

Client: I'm fat.
Therapist: How strongly do you believe this?
Client: Ninety percent.
Therapist: How does the thought affect your behaviour?
Client: I try to compensate in other ways—I overwork, I avoid men, I don't eat.
Therapist: How does the thought affect your emotions?
Client: I feel miserable. I lack confidence. I feel anxious.
Therapist: What evidence makes you believe the thought? (PROMPT) Past experience?
Client: Men don't compliment me. Mother said that my sister was attractive she didn't mention me.
Therapist: (PROMPT) School friends etc?
Client: I was never one of the in-crowd at school.
Therapist: (PROMPT) Fashion models? Cultural ideals?
Client: Whenever I see models I know I can't be like them.
Therapist: What evidence is there to suggest there may be other ways of looking at it? (PROMPT) Is there evidence that other people find you attractive?
Client: Well, I suppose Nigel did.
Therapist: (PROMPT) Physical attractiveness using a cultural model has a very narrow definition. What makes people attractive to you?
Client: I usually go for the personality above all else.
Therapist: If you asked other people their opinion of what you are saying, what would they say? (PROMPT) For a less extreme view. How would you summarise the facts now?
Client: I'm not as attractive physically as some women but more than others. Attractiveness is not just a physical attribute.
Therapist: How strongly do you believe this? How could you test out whether your conclusion is realistic? (PROMPT) Do you know an example of classic beauty who is unattractive? Do you know anyone who is not beautiful but is attractive?

However, sometimes work on this level can be understood by the head but doesn't reach the heart. It is important to explore in more detail the implication of shape and weight for your clients. It may be helpful to search within their autobiographical memory to find events which may resonate with their current disgust and shame with their shape and weight. Imagery to recall past events in more detail may be helpful:

- Can they imagine the time of their birth?
- How did each of their parents react to their arrival?
- What about the time they started secondary school or menarche?
- How were they judged then by other family members?

One of the most common maladaptive thoughts is that it is essential for them to be perfect in terms of physical attractiveness. Encourage them to read feminist literature which may help them moderate their attitude of themselves as objects. It may also be helpful to encourage them to read books which explicitly describe cultures in which women are treated as objects. (For example *Princess* by Jean Sasson about life for women in Saudi Arabia and *Wild Swans* by Jung Chang which describes several generations of women's lives in China.) Novels, films, poetry, etc., correspond best with this level of information-processing. The aim is to help your clients to question their own harsh self-schemata.

Also, during this stage it is useful to review the lifetime weight chart to check for links between weight loss and life events and difficulties. It is possible that current difficulties resonate with events and problems in the past and it can be helpful to make these links.

The maladaptive views of the self which are common in bulimia nervosa clients are:

- the need to be perfect
- the need to please others
- the need for control alternating with a spirit of rebelliousness
- a sense of defectiveness.

It is possible to address some of these issues in this short-term treatment but strongly fixed schemata will need more intensive psychotherapy.

INTERPERSONAL DIFFICULTIES

It may be that in treatment, you will identify severe deficits and problems with interpersonal relationships which are important triggers or maintaining factors. Worksheet 9, (*The Web of Life*, Appendix, p.CG85), can help focus on these issues. Once you have identified areas that seem to be important, explore the problem further using the skills of reflective listening. Remember to keep your focus on change of your clients' eating patterns which will probably also mean a change in their relationship to their social network.

Look at the obstacles to change in their relationships and examine whether there is any ambivalence about moving on. What are the difficulties that change will cause? Understanding and anticipating the nature and strength of these difficulties is important as you may be able to help them to consider alternative strategies for dealing with them.

Loss is an important triggering event for bulimia nervosa. The development of an eating disorder can interrupt the grieving process. Guided mourning may help in such cases. There may be ambivalence about grieving. For example, in order to realistically appraise the loss it may be necessary to look at negative aspects of the relationship as well as positive ones. The client may want to idealise the lost one and so is reluctant to consider anything other than perfection. Or there may be a fear that once they allowed themselves to feel the loss or the anger that they may become overwhelmed with emotion and never be able to stop crying or to feel calm again. It may be necessary to teach your client skills to deal with these intense emotions. The focus should be on trying to help the client to steer away from extreme positions but to be able to see good and bad in all things.

Giving information about the process of grieving is helpful as it normalises feelings of disbelief, sadness, anger and then acceptance, that are part of the process.

Relationship difficulties within the family can also act as antecedents, triggers or maintaining factors. There may be long-standing disputes. Reflective listening may help you understand why the conflict has not been resolved. What are the pros and cons of leaving the situation in the air? Once your clients can understand why they are stuck in that position then they may be able to use negotiation skills to try to move on.

Another common area of difficulty in these clients—because of their developmental age at the onset of their illness—is their need to readjust to a new role, for example, they may need to achieve independence from the family or perhaps marriage or parenthood. First help them clarify what they will have lost with their old role. Once this has occurred they can consider developing relationships and activities in the new role. A similar process to that involved in resolving grief is needed.

Others have long-standing difficulties in relationships with others and may alternate between being overdependent or being totally alone, or being abused or abusive. Clients with such manifest personality difficulties will require more specific interventions and will need to be referred on for further help.

TERMINATION OF TREATMENT

Approximately 40–50% of clients respond well to the short-term symptom-focused type of intervention described here. If you have reached the end of this stage and your client remains symptomatic then you need to reassess the situation. It is possible that personality difficulties or depression may have interfered with motivation. Consider again the use of an antidepressant. If personality difficulties appear to be the major block to progress, referral for psychotherapy should be considered. As outlined earlier, a variety of short-term therapies are now available.

RELAPSE PREVENTION

We found that following treatment with the self-help book *Bit(e) by Bit(e)* clients tended to continue to improve, whereas in some cases, clients who had had standard cognitive behavioural treatment relapsed at the three and six months follow-up. This suggests to us that the book is helpful in preventing relapse. Warn your clients that their eating disorder will be their Achilles heel and will tend to re-emerge at a time of stress for a long time to come. The most important thing is to realise that this is to be expected and does not have to be interpreted as being a catastrophe. For example, it is not as if they will never overcome their eating disorder because they have had a relapse. Remind them about the revolving door of change and indicate that each time they spin round the circle they will have gained more information. They will be able to prepare coping strategies for high-risk situations and be able to quickly instigate measures which will bring their eating under control. They may need to keep the book with them by their side for such moments.

The stages of change model is also useful as an antidote to therapist despair or burn-out. Therapeutic failure may be evidence that more work or maturing needs to happen before lasting improvement can occur. However, some clients may never be ready to change. There may be interpersonal difficulties or environmental hazards which require further work.

If even the additional forms of therapy outlined here are ineffective then consider alternatives. Frequently, it is useful to halt regular therapy but review progress as an outpatient. Alternative strategies are:

- start with a new therapist;
- admit for inpatient treatment;
- consider whether pharmacotherapy may help motivation.

CASE REPORT 1

In this section we will illustrate the use of motivational enhancement therapy with one of our clients. She was referred to the eating disorder clinic by her general practitioner. We include the written material that we gave her and also the written homework that she completed. Obviously, some details have been changed to preserve anonymity.

This client was very motivated when she first came for treatment. Do not despair if this seems too good to be true. We all have clients who are much less motivated than the one described here. The example of a client who is well motivated illustrates optimal use of the techniques we describe.

Susan

Susan was a 20-year-old woman with a four-year history of bulimia nervosa with laxative abuse and vomiting. At the end of the assessment session we offered her outpatient treatment which she accepted. She was given *Bite(e) by Bit(e)* and the *Workbook: Motivational Enhancement Therapy* (see Appendix, p.CG76) and we told her that we would use these to structure her treatment. We asked her to start looking through this material before her first session and to complete some of the exercises.

Session 1

The following is the feedback letter sent to her at the end of the first session.

Dear Susan,

You came to the Eating Disorder Unit because of concern about your eating disorder. You described it as ruining your health and we talked about this in more detail. You described getting weakness, cramp and pain after taking the laxatives. You were also vomiting frequently. Your psychological health is also deteriorating in that on occasions you drank large amounts of alcohol in order to avoid eating. When drunk you behave impulsively and on one occasion you almost jumped out of a train, and another time you pulled your hair out.

Your family life is also disturbed, your mother is extremely concerned about you and indeed your aunt came with you today. Your work, you say, is not really being impaired by your problems although you do know that when you went out drinking during the lunchtime you would come back rather tearful which would get noticed.

Another problem is that you are £2000 in debt mainly because you try to disguise going to buy laxatives amongst buying other products. Your social life has suffered in that you get less pleasure in going out with friends and you note that the idea of getting close to a boyfriend fills you with disgust.

Your weight has fluctuated over the last two or three years. Your weight was steady at 10½ stones and when you started work, at a time of stress, your weight went up to 13 stones. You have had four episodes where you have attempted to reduce your weight by laxatives or vomiting and fasting but each time you have relaxed your controls on this your weight has increased to between 12 and 13 stones.

You describe this present episode developing at a time when you changed your job and felt you took on more responsibility than you were prepared for and also at a time when you felt very let down by your first serious boyfriend.

You describe nothing abnormal in your early life although at middle school you were bullied because of acne, but your parents and your teachers did something about this and you also got medication from doctors. You are the middle of three children. You note that both your sister and father have quite a big build but very few other members of your family have had any weight-related problems.

You did well at school obtaining GCSEs and worked for a building society for four years. Your second job was more stressful and you needed appraisals every month but since you moved into your current job you are much happier.

In conclusion, you have developed bulimia nervosa and this has been complicated by overconsumption of alcohol and risk-taking behaviour and it has profoundly affected your physical health and in particular your social life and your family are extremely concerned about this. You have managed to reduce your laxative consumption but in some ways this has just been replaced by vomiting. We have given you a book and a workbook and hope that you can work with these with your therapist to make some progress on your eating disorder. We are very impressed with the warmth and concern of your family. Before your first appointment it would be helpful if you could do some of the exercises described.

(*Supervisor:* This letter highlights and reflects back many of the negative things about bulimia nervosa that were elicited in the assessment interview. There was then an attempt to formulate the problem and to define triggering factors—in this case the transition to a new job after failing in one and the loss of a boyfriend. The childhood antecedents appeared to be surprisingly mild—bullying, which was effectively dealt with. Maintaining factors were pronounced—rebound weight gain, once bulimic weight control measures were relaxed; and use of alcohol).

Therapist: The first thing I noticed about Susan when she walked in for her first session of therapy was her hair. It was long and extremely bushy and curly but was tied up at the back very unsuccessfully. Little bits had escaped from the rubber-band and lay in disarray round her ears. There were also short bits of hair, that I gathered from the assessment letter, were due to hair being pulled out. Susan was dressed, or rather covered up with, a large plum-coloured anorak which did very little to de-emphasise her rather pale, pasty complexion. As she walked in she placed in my hand her "homework" which was dated two days before our meeting. She had obviously completed the first few pages of the Workbook exercises in preparation for our first meeting.

Worksheet 2: Is Change Reasonable?
How does the bulimia boa constrictor affect you?

> Answer:
> *It rules my life sometimes when I can't keep it under control. It's keeping me locked away and not letting me out. I can't go out into public places very often as it tries to embarrass me. It's like my shadow and wherever I run to, it can keep up. I can't go to restaurants and nightclubs just in case I need to go to the loo, and everyone can hear me and smell what I'm doing. I can't be ME when it is there. My character changes and I become someone I don't even know. It knows me very well and can stop me doing all the things I love to do. It knows where and when to hit me the hardest, it will never let me go.*

(*Supervisor:* Susan is clearly able to articulate some of the concerns that she has about her bulimia nervosa, for example, social embarrassment and psychological impairment. However, she obviously has very little confidence that she can change. For example, it is as if the bulimia nervosa is inextricably bound up with her like a shadow.)

Worksheet 3: Difficulties of Change
What difficulties will you encounter when you start to struggle with your bulimia boa constrictor?

> Answer:
> *It's like a shadow and when I think its gone away, it will pop up at any moment to show me who is boss. I will have to have more courage and not be afraid. It will be like walking about naked and feeling like something is missing from me. I will be afraid of a lot more things and feel I can't hide my feelings from everyone so much. It*

*will feel like everybody will know that I'm weak and not in control
of myself. It will be laughing in my face waiting for me to fail so it
can take over again.*

(*Supervisor:* It appears from this that the bulimia nervosa helps to
cover up her feelings of nakedness—perhaps by this she means her
vulnerability. Underlying this may be her uncertainty about her
competence about changing her role into that of an independent mature
adult from a child. She also hints that the bulimia nervosa serves the
function of controlling her emotions.)

Worksheet 4: Future Times
How will you cope without your bulimia boa constrictor?

Answer:
*At first it will be as I said before (like feeling naked and afraid to
face the world on my own). But then, hopefully, I will feel like a free
person like there are better things in life waiting for me to see and
do. It would be great for me to keep it under control instead of it
keeping me under control. If I had my way I would lock it up in a
box and throw away the key forever. I will think that I have left
behind something that had me in control. It's part of me that needs
to be put into my past life and must stay there. I will probably learn
from it (I hope), and be a better person from having gone through it.
It will be hard but I must fight on and start to enjoy my life. I don't
class it as my friend. I class it as an evil side of me that wasn't letting
the good side come out into the daylight, and I think I can cope
without it. It's not going to rule.*

(*Supervisor:* This piece of work reveals a trace of optimism. There is
the possibility that Susan can recognise that the bulimia nervosa will
interfere with her long-term goals. On the other hand, there is no
realistic acknowledgement about how the change will occur. It is as if
there is a wish for a magic solution. A desire for a wizard to lock the
bulimia away in a box.

This exercise has brought out some self-motivating statements. For
example, the last part of the exercise beginning ... "I must fight on and
enjoy my life." The therapist should pick up on this statement, highlight
and affirm it. It is worth reading it back to her and saying how interesting you think it is. Ask her to comment on how she feels about it.

To summarise and feed back you might say: "It is obvious from your
thinking about this exercise that you are not certain about how you will

overcome your bulimia. You almost have a wish for a magical solution. As if you would like me to lock it away for you. What comes out strongly, and which is great, is the fact that you have clearly recognised bulimia nervosa as an enemy. You appear to be determined to put it behind you as you know that it is interfering with attaining important goals in your life. That is an excellent start to therapy. I have already seen your willingness to work in the way that you completed these exercises before we met.")

In addition to writing about the images of struggling with her bulimia, Susan had written the letters from Worksheets 2 and 3 (Appendix, pp.CG78 and CG79).

Letter to your *friend* Bulimia Nervosa

Dear Bulimia Nervosa,
Just wanted to say thanks for all your help with my life. You make me feel so much better when I'm down and you help me hide all those horrible feelings that I have deep down. You make me feel clean and fresh and happier when everything is going so very wrong. You help me get on with my life making things make sense, helping me to deal with them the only way I know how. You take control letting me sit back and relax. It's like you pick me up and carry me over the burning fire of worry and put me safely the other side, not letting anyone know what has gone on. You are brilliant. Maybe I should stay with you, you always make sense at the end of the day. You put a screen up so that I don't get hurt anymore. I know that you care for me more than anyone else. The last 4 years I have been turning to you and you never turned me away, not like a boyfriend that has had enough of you or when friends let you down all the time. You're just there, you don't have to say anything. I know what you are saying and that you are comforting me all the time. I know I get angry with you for always being here but you never get cross with me. You just show me the way ahead all the time.

(*Supervisor:* This letter describes the way that the bulimia is used to control emotions. Susan clearly articulates her use of bulimia nervosa as a coping device for dealing with distress and worry. This would suggest that one focus of treatment will be on skills to cope with distress. She also depicts bulimia nervosa as the perfect confidante. The therapist should begin to think about her social network, why has she no friends she can trust, what about her sister?)

Letter to your *enemy* Bulimia Nervosa

To Bulimia Nervosa,
*   You are getting in my way and I hate you for it. You think that*
you can rule me and my life. You are upsetting me and my family,
putting my mum and dad through hell and stopping any happiness
I have from getting out. You make my feelings run all over the place
making me feel sad and lonely wanting to end my life. You are very
evil and very hateful. If you had your way my life would be just an
existence but I'm going to fight you all the way to the end and I'm
going to win the battle.
*   You think that everything should be this way but it shouldn't. To*
me you're my enemy and you will stay that way always. I will go
out and have a good time and be MYSELF and I won't let you stop
me anymore, you are history! You play with my mind like a chess
game and you think you can get checkmate all the time and keep
me blocked. When I'm down you jump on me and cover me with all
your evil ways. Well, I'm telling you now this is it. I am starting to
fight back now and I'm going to give you a hard time. You are like
a secret that can't be told because you embarrass me too much. Your
life is over now and mine is going to be free from you forever and
ever.

(*Supervisor:* Again this letter has made Susan focus on the negative
aspects of her bulimia. She highlights the effect on her family and on
her psychological health. However, the letter is full of self-motivating
statements which follow "You are very evil and very hateful ..." These
statements are a gift to the therapist and should be emphasised and be
the basis of positive feedback from the therapist.)

Therapist: If I were to plot Susan's degree of motivation on Prochaska
and DiClemente's (1986) "five stages of change"—precontemplation,
contemplation, preparation, action and maintenance—she was nearing
the end of the "contemplation stage" and ready for the "preparation
stage". What she had not got were any of the skills or confidence so that
she could enter the action stage. On the other hand, she had been able
to define and convey to us some of the positive reinforcers for her bulimic
behaviour.

Susan was certainly able to express her feelings on paper but it was as
if emotions were not allowed. It was as if she was unable to describe or
accept why she was feeling hurt or rejected. Perhaps she had the

unrealistic expectation that if she allowed herself to experience a degree of loss or rejection she would become destroyed. She therefore attempted to blank off these emotions to put them behind a screen. It wasn't yet clear what her "dirty" feelings were like and it seemed too early to explore this in great detail in the first session. We would later have to consider how she could feel "clean" without having to purge. One particular problem she was struggling with was her ambivalence over wanting to be independent from her parents and yet fearing the consequences of having such freedom in that she might appear to others to be naked and vulnerable. She did appear to lack a trusted friend in her social network and used bulimia nervosa to fulfil this function.

A second problem was the somewhat ironical double-bind in which she became involved, as a member of a close family. How, in fact, could she share her suffering with those in the family who were already suffering through watching her? This was where I thought the therapeutic alliance would be helpful: to become for Susan a close, but compassionate "outsider" who could symbolically "hold her" as she told her story in detail but who could retain an overall perspective.

This first meeting then revolved around two main issues. The first focused on Susan's ambivalence over independence and needing protection. The second involved the use of bulimia as a means of controlling feelings. It appeared as if she used alcohol to fulfil the same function as bulimia nervosa. With a view to seeing if there were any parallels between bulimia and alcohol I gave Susan some homework, which was to describe what effects both bulimia and alcohol had on her. I also asked her to work on the letters to a friend on Worksheet 4 (Appendix, p.CG80).

Effects of Alcohol when You Are Depressed

I think it is like sitting on a time bomb waiting to go off. The drink is flowing and everyone is having fun. You are laughing and joking and thinking you are having a good time but the question is: are you?! You are feeling very drunk and emotions are running very high, suddenly you are feeling very low and tearful. You know that everyone can tell the way your mood swing has gone. They start asking you what is wrong. You say "nothing" in a voice that makes out everything is OK but really you just want to be alone and cry your heart out, you don't even know why. You start thinking that life is very hard on you and it's not worth living anymore. You go quiet and withdrawn, you don't understand yourself, WHY?

You are going home on your own. Your mind is racing over all the embarrassing things you have said and done that night. You feel sad and very unhappy. This is a danger sign when you feel this low. It is times like these that could be the last of your lifetime.

(*Supervisor:* This appears to confirm the therapist's ideas that Susan used alcohol as a mood regulator. However, Susan has some recognition of how it backfired on her with very serious consequences.)

Write a letter to a friend describing your life in 5 years' time when you have recovered from bulimia nervosa:

Dear Friend,
Hi, I'm feeling great with myself, I feel my life is only just beginning. I had bulimia nervosa 5 years ago and at the time I thought that was the way I should live my life but now I feel great. I have a healthy lifestyle with swimming and surfing. I can go out in public places and to restaurants and nightclubs, having a great time with my friends. I have even been on holiday for the first time in years. I feel on top of the world. I even eat a healthy diet which got me to a weight of 9½ stone. I have toned up my body and can even go out in vest tops and swimming suits and feel great about myself. I have met a new man and he thinks the world of me. He even knows about the illness I had and said it doesn't bother him one bit—isn't that great? I'll tell you something—I even love myself the way I am and can do all sorts of things like look at myself in the mirror without any clothes on and say to myself "you look great" and really mean it. When my man says I look good I know he means it and that he is not just saying it because it will make me feel better. Oh, I feel great, I can't describe that feeling but it's damn good.

(*Supervisor:* This letter contains many self-motivating statements and clearly sets out her long-term goals. You might want to feed back how great it is that Susan can so clearly visualise the future. On the other hand, the letter does almost seem too good to be true. We can't all live the life of a glossy magazine girl. Perhaps it is worth pointing this out to her, gently.)

Write a letter to a friend describing your life in 5 years' time when you still have bulimia nervosa:

Dear Friend,
Hi, I'm feeling OK. Life has been a bit hard on me lately, I am always feeling tired and sleeping a lot of the time. I have lost contact with a few of my friends and haven't been out very much. I'm hoping

*to go on holiday but I have to be a lot slimmer to go on the beach
and for everyone to see me. Then again, I think I won't go. I have a
lot of backache and have to rest a lot, but I feel OK today. I can't get
over how cold I feel all the time at the moment and it's lovely weather.
I have even got an electric blanket on my bed because I feel so cold.
Some friends invited me out for a meal last week but I didn't go
because I was feeling very tired and a bit down. But I shouldn't talk
about me all the time—how are you getting on? Are you going on
holiday this year? I will come up and see you soon, I know it's been
2 years but I have been so busy with work and everything—you know
how it is. Anyway, I don't have very much more to write so I'll let
you know when I'm coming to see you, OK?*

(*Supervisor:* One of the most interesting parts of this letter is how
Susan expresses the painfulness of continuing with bulimia nervosa.
She is able to define how the bulimia nervosa will interfere with her
goals. She will not be able to go on holidays and it will cut her off from
friends.)

Session 2

Therapist: During this session we covered many aspects of Susan's
bulimia nervosa. There were, for example, the more painful, emotional
and/or psychological aspects like:

- *why* was she bingeing, vomiting, taking laxatives and/or drinking;
- *how* (or whether) these methods were successful in helping her to feel
  better about herself;
- *what* other "means" could she use to communicate her feelings?

During the session we looked for alternative ways of soothing and
comforting herself in the face of distress. We practised active skills to
stop the distress caused by "doormat"-type, pleasing behaviour. This
included role-playing. We discussed how "shoulds" could be eliminated
from dialogue or thinking substituting things like "I would rather...." or
"When you do such and such I feel ....".

I considered that Susan was moving into the action phase and so I
decided to include skills to stop the bulimia directly. We therefore
discussed more practically based and educationally informative issues.
For example, we looked at her "diet" and saw how depriving herself of
nourishing and/or sufficient food made her want to compensate by
bingeing. I then asked Susan to keep a diary of what she ate and, if she
binged, to say something about what she did and how she felt about it.
This is what Susan wrote:

MONDAY, 7.30 PM

Food for the day:
Yoghurt low fat
Jacket potato with lettuce and coleslaw
2 slices of white bread and marmite and low fat spread

What was eaten on binge:
3 yoghurts low fat
2 doughnuts
3 cooked sausages
2 cream cakes

30 minutes after a binge:
Well, you have got me at last. I thought I could fight you but you won. I feel like you're back in control of me and it's hurting me. I don't know why you're making me cry. I'm sitting over the toilet throwing up all that bad food and you are laughing in my face. My hands are shaking and I'm very scared at this moment in time. I will take laxatives tonight, it will make my head spin. I will feel clean but sad this time. You are saying "It's OK, don't worry". I'm calm and peaceful now. It's strange, one minute I'm crying and my hands are shaking and now only minutes later I feel total control. It's not all of me here but I'm happy in a weird sort of way. Numb is the word to say how I'm feeling now. Hello, Bulimia Nervosa.
5 laxatives were taken.
I was up 4 times in the early hours of the morning.
Today I feel empty.

Therapist: Susan read out what she had written in her diary. However, what she had not written about was why she had binged. She told me during the session that her new boyfriend Richard had discovered a copy of *Bit(e) by Bit(e)* in her handbag and ever since then had been acting very "cool" and distant towards her. Eventually she realised that he could not deal with the fact that she had an eating disorder and he no longer wanted to continue the relationship. We focused on two particular issues. The first related to how Susan interpreted his "rejection" of her. I tried to get her to consider alternative ways of looking at the situation. Was he really rejecting her or was she threatening him because he did not want to deal with (his own?) emotional issues? I focused on how Susan could try to clarify the communication rather than block off from it using her bulimia, leaving him to continue to distance himself. I suggested that Susan wrote a letter to Richard describing how she felt about his actions. Here is how she tackled this homework assignment:

Dear Richard,

I just wanted to clear a few things up. I know that there is a lot of difference between us. At first I couldn't see it but as time goes on I can see that it was best for us to part because of mixed up feelings. I hope that everything is going better for you and that your life has become a lot easier. At the end of our short relationship it was like trying to keep a dying flower alive and that is impossible. I was holding on for some spark that just wasn't there. I have heard you are going back to your old girlfriend and I wish you both all the best. I hope that the difficulty at work will become a lot easier on the both of us. I don't hold any grudges towards you and hope that we can talk again as we used to and not feel so uncomfortable with the situation. I will always care for you because of all the special times we spent together and that is mine to keep forever. If I had my way I would have turned back the clock and met you 6/12 months after you finished with your girlfriend instead of meeting you so soon after you split up with her but that's life. I would like to thank you for the great times we had and wish you all the happiness for the future. I hope this clears the air between us and then we can both get on with our lives.

With love,
Susan

Therapist: The episode with Susan and her boyfriend Richard represented some kind of watershed in her therapy. In the main we pursued the two themes that had already arisen, that is, on the one hand, Susan's conflicts about wanting control and/or independence, and on the other, fearing the loss of such control and independence. Although her relationship with Richard was different from that with her parents there were similarities, especially relating to Susan's dependence on him to make her feel good about herself and to cover up her "nakedness". In other words, Susan, perhaps like many other women, needed a relationship for its own sake, rather than one that satisfied her own needs and wants. In fact, in order to develop real independence, Susan needed to value herself for herself.

We also reviewed Susan's tendency to polarise feelings and judgements, and how she had demonstrated in her letter to Richard that she was able to change this. What impressed me most about this letter was how she was able to retain all the good things about the relationship as well as "clearing the air" or saying what she had to say. This was a far cry from the person who had no control and was "… sitting over the toilet throwing up all that bad food" which she began to see represented "bad (or unexpressed) feelings".

Sessions 3–7

During these sessions we looked at how bulimia nervosa was used to control distress and, in turn, how interpersonal relationships caused distress. I helped Susan to link current and past experiences. I also explored how the solution to distress had been to focus on weight and appearance.

Session 8

Susan came to this session equipped with a file she had been compiling regarding her newly found "confidence". She told me that she had begun to realise that people did not look at her when she walked into a room in order to judge her looks. Now that she had become more reflective about herself, and people in general, she had discovered that everyone was more interested and/or preoccupied with their own concerns. She came to realise then that her assumptions about what they had been thinking about represented her own projections.

During this session Susan broke down at one moment because she had a "dark secret". She had been wanting to tell me about it but had never as yet been able to. This involved an experience she had had as a child which she had never told to anyone other than to her mother. Susan's pain was overwhelming. She could not even describe the event and I was left to speculate over and over again, eventually succeeding in articulating it for her. Once she had affirmed it I could help her to remove it from the dark and place it into the light, with humour providing an even warmer glow. In all, I do believe that the telling of the tale provided its own healing.

Towards the end of this session Susan and I discussed the termination of therapy. The plan had been for Susan to have a maximum of 16 sessions. Susan felt she had gone as far as she wanted, and needed to, and I asked her to bring her goodbye letter to me for the next session. I cite my letter to her, which was an attempt to formulate her problem.

Dear Susan,

We have now had 8 sessions. Looking back to your first session when you came to see me, it is quite difficult to believe that you are the same person. You have now not taken any laxatives for about 5 weeks; your one relapse having been 5 weeks ago. Not only have you not taken any laxatives but you seem so much more confident. You are also looking so much healthier, your hair is shining and your skin looks good.

You had written in your letter that you were "frightened to face the world" without your bulimia. You said that it "felt like being naked". Despite this you have managed, subsequent to your one relapse, which seems to have been precipitated by the break-up with your then boyfriend, to recover. You were able (quite impressively I thought) to write and tell him what you were feeling and, in addition, you were able to carry on and have some kind of relationship with him, even though it was not a romantic one. I thought that was very courageous of you and I applaud you for it.

Around about the same time as you sent this letter you had a discussion with your mother when you told her that you were thinking of moving out of home, in the main because as you said, you wanted to be independent, to be able to do what you liked when you liked, not to "have to talk to anyone if you did not want to". When I asked you what you would do if there was no one at the other end of the phone, you said that you would phone someone else. Whilst I feel that it was a very big step for you to have this kind of talk with your mother, particularly when you were able to be affectionate with her (which as you said has not been the case for some time), I do feel somehow that what we have not discussed enough is: Where is that side of you that may still feel somewhat "naked" and "quite frightened to face the world" on your own?

Perhaps there is a danger that you may, Susan, be used to looking at yourself in very extreme terms. Either you feel vulnerable and frightened and there is a real chance of the bulimia coming back. As you put it, it is "like a shadow" and can attack you when you least expect it. Or else, you feel ready to go out and live completely on your own. In other words, you seem uncertain—and indeed we have not spent much time discussing the more "grey areas"; what it means to be both vulnerable and independent; to be both confident and not confident. But perhaps more importantly, to be able to understand that seeing that other people "are not so perfect" is not necessarily going to help you with your self-confidence. I am referring in particular to our discussion last week when you told me how you were now able to see that there were people who did not have (including your sister Diana who you admire so much) some of your good qualities, like lovely hair, etc.

Now whilst this seems a big step for you as you have always seen yourself, as you tell me, in very inferior terms to others, I feel that the next step for you must be to like yourself for what you are, rather than for being "better than" others. And I feel that part of liking yourself for what you are is to come to terms with the many sides of you, good and bad, likeable and not so likeable. This would include the Susan who may not be so good at maths; the Susan who may some of the time be quite frightened to be all alone in a flat; the Susan who may not be liked by everyone. But also, this would include the Susan who has been very courageous, has worked hard to try and understand herself and who has achieved so much, particularly, it has to be said, in regard to communicating better with your family and friends, in addition to adopting a more "normal" style of eating.

I do think that you have a tendency to value yourself too much in terms of how you look. What this suggests to me is that you have not sufficiently taken to heart your other qualities and attributes. This sounds like there might be another circle here: either you try to get other people to like you so that you don't have to think about why you like yourself. But then when you do think about yourself you do not think too deeply. Instead, you focus on just "your outer shell". But, Susan, I think you are more than this outer shell and I also think that you know it somehow. (Indeed, perhaps it might be a worthwhile thing for you to look in a more concentrated way on the deeper aspects of yourself like, for example, your creativity?)

To sum up: I still think overall that your next goal must be to look beyond your outer shell and look more at what is inside the shell, even if it means taking both the good and the bad, the vulnerable and the independent.

Session 9

Therapist: Susan forgot to bring her goodbye letter to me with her but promised to post it. As I sat next to Susan I remember looking at a pink-cheeked young woman with curly, bushy hair, let loose, and instead of a large anorak she wore a smart jacket with a pencil skirt.

During this session we not only reviewed the therapy but also came up with some additional insights. The first of these was to do with her sister, Diana.

Susan used to view her as the sister she envied; who had "everything"; an extroverted personality, able to say whatever she liked, etc. Now Susan saw how maybe this was a "front" to deal with the excessive "fussing" that she seems to have felt she had as a child. I drew a map for her showing how this "pattern" established itself. It went something like "I am fragile, in need of fussing"—"I get fussed over". Then as Susan got older, when she had more "knowledge" and/or vocabulary, the "I am fragile, need fussing over" became more, as Susan put it, "exaggerated". What I interpreted her as saying was that she found herself working harder at maintaining the "being fragile/being fussed over behaviour". We then completed the cycle by reviewing what was happening when the bulimia began. It was interesting to reflect on the polarised thoughts and actions, culminating in ambivalence: that is, "I am getting big now I can't bear to be fussed over." "Being fussed over means I have no control." But on the other hand, "fussing may be the only way that I have of gaining mummy's love."

However, this ambivalence was further exacerbated by yet another pattern that was establishing itself. This time it was connected with the "rewards" she was getting from others about "how great she looked". As Susan described it the "rewards" (my words) were overpowering but at the same time, no one really knew what was going on. Susan says it was so easy to form a whole fantasy world. In it she was not only "eating all right" but "going out with lots of guys". "You can say anything you want" she told me "when you have this fantasy world". I then asked her what the downside was and she described it as if "there was no one there". When I asked her what she meant she said that there was no person there and even if someone like her present boyfriend, Peter, had arrived on the scene, there would have been "no one there to have a relationship with". We then spoke about Peter and I told her about my concerns about her seeing him as "saviour" rather than as (as she put it) "icing on the cake". I really felt that she knew what I was inferring.

We spoke a great deal, finally, about the possibility of a relapse but I really do feel confident that if she does have one she will be in a much better position to deal with it. I have really enjoyed working with Susan, in the main, because she was so motivated to get better. After this session the therapist took the (in our practice unusual step) to send the client a further letter, addressing some of the issues that had emerged in this last session.

This was the therapist's goodbye letter:

Dear Susan,

I feel we have come a long way together and yet it's only 4 months since you first came to see me. During that time we have looked at many aspects of your life. If I had to say which "one" was the most important I think it would be how you used to bottle-up your feelings. I guess the most surprising and welcoming thing by far was just how hard you worked on this and in a space of a few weeks you could see how much easier it was to open up and say where it hurts. If you remember, it was very soon after you told me how you got close to your mother that you came in and told me that you felt you had been mistaken about your feeling that "other people" had confidence; that is, everybody but you! You then said that you realised now that everyone needed to work on confidence: ALL THE TIME. I hope you will remember this!

Looking back again to our sessions together, and again if I had to say when I really believed you had turned the corner, it was when you told me how you had begun to fear death and/or what you may or may not have done to your body with the laxatives. I know this sounds morbid but it was not. I saw it as one of the most positive things you were able to say up until that point. I say this, Susan, remembering that at your worst time you were taking 120 laxatives a day and you even said to me one day when you were feeling low that maybe you "were addicted to them". I wonder if you still think that is the case?

I am really happy for you that you have this new relationship and that it seems to be going well. Perhaps what I feel most pleased about is the belief that "if" anything should go wrong with it and it happens to end, that you will be in a better position to cope with it. I think you have learnt over the past 4 months how to share feelings and having that resource can make you so much stronger.

I am also pleased with how you have managed to look at your relationship with Diana and see how feelings for, or about people, are seldom one-way. I think that it does make a difference to realise that you can never be responsible for everything on the one hand, and on the other hand, that other people have their vulnerabilities too.

I am also pleased that we were able to "touch" on that very painful episode in your life which you were adamant you did not want to explore any further. I feel that we looked at it as much as you wanted to and I respect your judgement on that. I also respect your judgement on the fact that you have gone altogether as far as you want to go in therapy and that there are certain things, as you put it, which "are behind you".

We have made a date in the future to see each other for a follow-up session. But in the meantime, I would like to say to you how much I have enjoyed working with you and also that I will miss you.

All the best and keep sharing yourself,

This is the goodbye letter that Susan sent to her therapist:

Dear Marion,

I feel I have made the right choice to finish my sessions earlier than originally planned. At the start of our sessions I just couldn't see me getting any better—I thought I would be like this for life, everything looked so black and facing up to the road ahead was frightening. I feel a changed person. I am getting to know myself again and learning about who I was before I had bulimia.

Life has a lot more meaning and I'm starting to see things through both sides (black/white). I am getting on better with my friends and family, which I feel is a great improvement, opening up and letting out how I feel isn't as bad as I thought it might be. I feel there is a lot ahead of me in life and feel I have wasted 4 years due to bulimia. In my sessions with you I have learnt to understand myself a lot better (e.g. feelings, emotions), things I couldn't see about myself, when everyone else could.

My relationship with my sister has improved a lot. I don't feel so threatened by her being with me and coming out with my friends. We both have lots of different qualities and I can see this much more clearly. I am thinking of how Diana feels as well as myself. I didn't look at things through Diana's eyes, I was only seeing them through mine. I'm taking things as a whole not just looking at the outside but the inside as well.

Talking about my childhood made me understand what I was like. I feel the time when I was 9 until 11 was the hardest part to talk about, I just couldn't bring myself to face up to what had happened, I had buried it for so long I thought I could lock it away and never have to face it again, but thanks to you I can see that I was young and all little children do things to find out about themselves.

Mum and I are getting on so much better. I can hug her without feeling embarrassed and feeling that this is the right time to hug. I do it because I want to. We sit down and chat and I can talk openly to her.

Peter and I have a great relationship too. We get on very well and I enjoy being with him. We express how we feel openly and talk about all sorts of things. I don't feel afraid of the breaking up of this relationship as I feel I'm on top of myself and I know when there is danger, when before I didn't.

Thank you very much for all your help. When I see danger points I will put our work into practice. Thank you again.

Love Susan

A few months later Susan wrote again to her therapist:

Dear Marion,
I just wanted to tell you how I'm getting on. I have been very busy which is a very good thing. I have forgotten I even had an illness.

My life is so different, I can stand up and say I'm enjoying my life to the full.

I was 21 in July and had a party with everyone there. I had lots of lovely presents and got a lot of attention and I was made to feel very special. I'm still with my boyfriend, Peter, and we are getting on very well. We have a good healthy relationship and I feel in control of myself and my body. We can go out for meals without me getting worried about what I eat.

At first it was hard but I now feel there are a lot more things in life than the way your body looks. I love myself the way I am and I am very proud of that fact. It took me a long time to face the fact that I will never be skinny but did I really want to be like a stick and look like the walking dead!!! I wouldn't have been where I am now.

I went on holiday in August and enjoyed myself very much. I was very good with my eating habits and made sure I had breakfast, dinner and tea. I didn't feel worried about my body and just got on and enjoyed myself. I had 4 lovely friends with me and we all got on very well. Here's a picture of the 5 of us having a good time.

I have been to Alton Towers with Peter and his brother, Chris, and girlfriend, Zoe. We went on all the rides and had a good laugh. It's nice to get on with each other's family.

Mum and I are closer than ever. We make a point of sitting down and talking about what has happened in the week. She says this is the happiest she has seen me in ages and it's not just because of Peter. Mum and I understand each other so much better than before. She knows when I need my space and when I want to be alone. I'm still at home but saving for a place of my own. I won't move out for a few years.

On the 25th of September I lost my gran who I was very close to. It's the first time I have had to deal with something grey in my life since not seeing you. I didn't keep my feelings locked up the way I used to. I cried and grieved with everyone else who knew my granny. I did at first start eating for comfort and have put on half a stone but I feel confident that I will get this under control. Mum saw the danger signs but we have talked about it and we both feel that I'm in control of the situation.

Diana is not doing so good. She's very low and I think it's because she is not happy with the way her life is. She hasn't got a boyfriend and her job is getting her down. I'm standing by her as she did for me. I can see when Diana is feeling low a lot better than I did before. I am very lucky because I have a very close relationship with my family. We all stick together through thick and thin. This showed up greatly when my granny died, we all held each other up to fight on.

I would like to thank you for all your help in getting me to where I am now. I can't describe how happy I am. I know it's your job and it must be so rewarding, you helped me rebuild my life. I know I will have this disorder lurking around for the rest of my life but I know now how to control it and I'm forever grateful. I know I have an appointment with you some time at the end of October / early November. Please could you let me know the exact date, thanks.

Best Wishes
Love Susan

Report on the 3-month Follow-up Session

It was extremely rewarding to see how happy and healthy Susan looked. I told Susan that I was sorry to hear about her granny dying. This seemed to give her the opportunity to talk about her feelings and I was impressed with how she had coped. She told me how she had been very close to her grandmother and that, for a while after her death, she had resorted to comfort eating. In all she had put on half a stone. However, what impressed me, apart from the fact that she did not take any laxatives, was that she was able to share not only her feelings with her family but also that she was able to share their feelings. When I told her how impressed I was that she had not taken laxatives again she said she was determined not to have to "go through with all that pain again". This fact alone was enough of a deterrent. Susan then told me how, after a short period of comfort eating, she went back to eating "normally" again, and she found that she lost the weight gained without even noticing it.

However, she discovered that since she has stopped taking laxatives that she is not "very regular". We talked about her diet and I recommended more wholemeal products, in particular taking a cereal like Allbran. I then asked her if the thought of going through all the pain, in regard to stopping taking laxatives, was the only thing that prevented her from resorting to them. She then said that she thought another important factor had been her discovery that talking about feelings was very good for her, that it prevented things accumulating "inside" when the only way out was to "get rid of them".

I decided to ask her if she ever thought about the one incident in her childhood which may very well have influenced her (now past) tendency to keep things to herself. In particular, I was interested in how she would react if she experienced anything in her present life which reminded her of this incident. My question was "would she be able to manage it or would she over-react?" Susan seemed to feel that the very fact that she could tell just one person who could "explain" it to her, and reassure her that she was not the only person who had had such an experience, was enough. But now, she said she wanted to "put it behind her".

This case is a clear example of how, if the patient is motivated, therapy progresses smoothly.

CASE REPORT 2

This client was seen by the same therapist, at the same time and with the same supervisor, yet her level of motivation and the progress made in treatment were very different. Why should this be the case? There are obvious differences in the prognostic features. Case 2 had a much longer history, with many previous attempts at treatment. However, what is interesting is how the process of therapy differs so much between the two cases. There are many important lessons to be learnt from this. Exponents of audit have a phrase that is useful in these situations: "Every mistake is a treasure."

Mary

Mary was in her forties and had had an eating disorder for many years. Her weight had fluctuated between 6½ and 10½ stones. When she came to the clinic her weight was 8 stones 12 pounds. Ideally, she wanted to weigh 8 stones, and so she considered herself to be very overweight. She binged and vomited several times per day and took approximately 25 laxative tablets on a daily basis. Over the years she had seen various psychologists and psychiatrists for her problem. Mary was referred to our unit by her occupational health physician.

Here is the letter written to her after the first meeting:

Dear Mary,
    You came to the Eating Disorder Clinic after you had seen your doctor and she requested that you came to a specialist clinic. You are not sure how appropriate or helpful this will be.
    (Concerns about Eating Disorder)
    You have several problems that are of concern to you. You tire easily and have frequent headaches. You often have cold hands and feet and your teeth are sensitive with receding gums. Your stomach often feels swollen.
    You describe your mood as subdued and you have poor concentration and memory. You are very isolated because you cannot eat with friends and you cannot invite people to your house because of the chaos there. You think your eating disorder played a large part in the break-up of your previous relationship. All your money goes on food.

(Triggers of Eating Disorder)

Your illness started when you went away to a very austere boarding school at the age of 11. You were caned on your first day there. Every day you had to get up early, wash in cold water and cover the basin with a towel in case anyone saw the dirty water. You had to flatten yourself against the wall when a nun passed.

When you became ill a doctor suggested that you returned home, but you felt this was impossible to do because you were aware of the expense that had been incurred by your family in sending you to the school. Your condition worsened after you had disappointing results in your O levels and your mother responded very critically to this.

(Antecedent Factors)

You describe your mother as very domineering, critical and controlling of you. You felt that she always had the expectation of high standards for you. This was particularly difficult for you as she was your teacher at school during part of your schooling. Your father had depression and alcohol problems. You are the oldest of 8 brothers and sisters.

You were sensitised to weight issues at an early age. You describe an episode of humiliation as a child when your mother felt that you had put on a lot of weight and took you to a chemist shop commenting to all and sundry, "look at her, I have got to weigh her".

You are troubled by slowness. This is related to what you describe as your perfectionism and your obsessionality. This meant that your grades in exams were poor and you took what you described as "a low grade course, at a low grade university". You had to repeat the course. You have had a variety of jobs some of which involved teaching English as a foreign language.

You married at the age of 30 after a long courtship. You describe your former husband as a selfish, sometimes sadistic man. Indeed, you describe him as a torturer. Your second important relationship was with a student of yours and in the end you felt deceived and cheated by him.

Despite your long history of eating difficulties and various treatment attempts, you obviously recognise your difficulties and have come for further help. You are able to give a clear history about your difficulties. I have given you a a copy of Bit(e) by Bit(e) which contains information that others have found helpful. One of our therapists will get in touch with you to start a course of treatment.

(*Supervisor:* The letter gives a detailed summary of Mary's complex and painful life story. It clearly states Mary's ambivalence and passivity about treatment in the opening paragraph, yet it ignores some important information. Mary was referred to the clinic by her occupational health physician. This makes it likely that she came for the assessment to some extent under "duress", and it would have been helpful if the assessing health professional had addressed this. The letter ends with a statement that Mary will be offered treatment. It is as if at this point the assessor is responding to Mary's desperately unhappy life story, rather than to keep in mind her ambivalence. The therapist then follows on from here in the first session firming up on the offer of treatment, instead of checking on her level of ambivalence.)

Session 1

Therapist: I set the rules for therapy and indicated that Mary would have 16 sessions. I offered her the choice of going over the assessment letter or starting afresh. Although she indicated that several details in the assessment letter were incorrect she did not take the opportunity to expand on this. Instead, she opted to make a fresh start describing herself on her own terms rather than going over the letter with the therapist. She told me that her past therapy had concentrated too much on "the psychological" to the detriment of "the physical". I started to discuss daily patterns of eating in detail. Mary asked for a diet plan but then complained that what was suggested was too much.

Mary then spontaneously volunteered that she had very little motivation for therapy. She had no confidence that anything would work because she had had several attempts at treatment in the past and all of them had failed. She then began to cry saying that it was all too painful. I ended by asking Mary to write some letters as homework.

(*Supervisor:* It is interesting that Mary did not want to read the assessment letter with her therapist. It seems that she felt very exposed by having her life story revealed in a letter. Her wish to focus on "the physical" instead of on "the psychological" reflects this.

The therapist responded to Mary's unease and pain by trying very hard to please her and by attempting to do what she thought the patient wanted. The therapist thus rushed straight into the action phase, suggesting changes in Mary's pattern of eating, without considering Mary's stage of change or allowing for the possibility that Mary might not be ready to move into action. However, the therapist's suggestion of action then led to increasing resistance from Mary who alternatively responded by giving "yes but" answers or dissolving into tears. Mary's open criticism of other treatments she had received in the past wrong-footed the therapist further and pushed her more into trying increasingly harder to be a perfect therapist focusing on action and completely losing her capacity to think in motivational terms. It was clearly a mistake to have given the homework assignments at the end of the session, as at that point Mary had obviously moved back into the precontemplation phase after tentatively entering, for a short period, the contemplation phase.

The therapist picked up that the session had gone poorly, as she wrote in her notes that she was concerned that Mary might not attend for further treatment. Thus, the therapist had accurately cued into the client's uncertainty of treatment but had failed to tackle this in a motivational manner.

With the wisdom of hindsight Mary should probably not have been given the offer of 16 sessions of treatment after a one-off assessment. Instead, a prolonged assessment of several sessions would have been helpful which would have allowed to look in some more detail at why she came for treatment and explore her ambivalence about treatment and collaboration with the therapist.)

Lesson to Be Learnt

The most important lesson here is that ambivalence about treatment needs to be first on the agenda. Things went wrong, because this somehow got lost in the transition from assessment to treatment.

It may be useful in this context to think of the problems that clients present to you by using the image of an onion that has layer upon layer. Motivational techniques may be needed to dissect through to the next layer. You need to develop skills to tune into any ambivalence or conflict when you pick it up. During the initial phases of treatment this will centre on conflict about getting therapeutic help, then it moves on to ambivalence about losing symptoms, then it will centre on ambivalence about tackling interpersonal difficulties.

Session 2

Mary started by apologising for her "depression" the previous week. She excused herself by saying that she had been "premenstrual". The session was spent discussing Mary's family history and early development. One of the earliest memories Mary recalled was being in her cot with her mother hitting her head with a ruler until she could recite her alphabet correctly. She recalled how difficult it was when she was in her mother's class at school. Her mother appeared to bend over backwards to avoid showing any favouritism. All the other children were called by their christian names but Mary was called "Miss Marles". She also described how several of her younger siblings suffered physical or sexual abuse by people outside the family.

(*Supervisor:* Mary has switched from being critical and rejecting in the first session to being pleasing to the therapist in the second session. It is as if she is giving the therapist what she thinks she wants (i.e. details of adverse events in childhood.)

Session 3

The next session was spent discussing Mary's relationship with her former husband. They had met in their teens but did not get married until she was 30. He often criticised her about her weight. She described the strategies of their courtship which involved her following, then leaving him until eventually he proposed. He would often comment that she had pursued him and forced him into marriage.

Mary had again failed to do any homework but would disarm the therapist by saying that it was too painful and her eyes would well up with tears. The therapist offered to go through it in the session. Mary would sit quietly sobbing and the therapist would ask gentle probing questions.

(*Supervisor:* In this session Mary clearly related the extreme positions of closeness, then distance, that she enters into with important interpersonal relationships. This is in exact parallel to what is going on in the relationship with her therapist.)

Session 4

Mary started by indicating that she had reduced her laxative tablets from 25 to 18 per day. When the therapist started to praise her for this, she downplayed her achievement saying that she had done it many times before. She discussed how hard she had found the weekend because of feeling very lonely. This led into a discussion about her former husband. She described him as if his character was a great contrast to her own and linked feeling unloved by him to being unloved by her mother.

(*Supervisor:* In this session Mary appears to be continuing to please her therapist by reducing her symptoms and by making links between the past and the present.)

Session 5

Mary had continued with taking fewer laxative tablets despite physical discomfort. In this session the therapist described the negative aspects of bulimia which included a disrupted education and a job below her abilities. When the therapist touched on the function that bulimia served to ward off loneliness Mary became tearful.

She and the therapist started to paint a more balanced picture of the relationship with her former husband. Mary indicated that he would cook for her and would go to a great deal of trouble and was saddened when she would vomit it all up. Mary was able to discuss the ways in which her behaviour could have appeared rejecting to him.

Session 6

Mary had been on holiday with her sister and had stopped vomiting because she felt she would be detected. However, while Mary was away changes were made in staffing at work so that Mary's job demands changed dramatically. Mary discussed all of this in a passive way.

The therapist, however, became very active and animated during this session. The therapist drew a picture of a cage and suggested that it was as if Mary was trapped in it. The therapist took an active role in leading a discussion into ways that Mary could escape from this cage.

(*Supervisor:* Again we can see how Mary's helpless, hopeless stance leads the therapist to actively try to help her. The therapist continues to rush into action without stopping to see whether she has Mary with her. Mary has a continuing difficulty in relationships in which she alternates between being a passive "victim" or a critical "abuser". This is the result of an underlying interpersonal schema which centres around the belief that: "If I become close to others they will humiliate and abuse me.")

Therapeutic work on this kind of schema is difficult as most of the cognitive processing is unconscious.

Session 7

Mary did not attend this session.

Session 8

Mary explained how she had missed the session the week before because she had overslept. She dismissively described the pay rise she had received at work. The therapist asked what she thought her needs were. She came up with "job satisfaction" and "recognition". The rest of the session was spent discussing her relationship with her father who was very distant throughout their childhood. He had spent most of his free time drinking with friends and played little part in the household other than to provide discipline when he did come home.

Session 9

Mary described her difficulties at work in which she felt as if she was being left out and sidelined. Her bulimic symptoms had returned. The therapist continued to look after her in this session, discussing her food and also reflecting on past difficulties and her response to them. The therapist asked her to do homework by writing a letter to her father.

Session 10

Mary again had failed to do her homework. She also described being left on her own in her flat and then going out to binge. The therapist became very active trying to work with Mary on alternative behaviours she could undertake when in this situation.

The therapist continued to make links between her pattern of relationships in her adult life with those in childhood, such as with her boss at work for whom she put in very long hours and yet never felt valued. For homework the therapist asked Mary to write down the messages she had received about the world as a child.

Session 11

Again, Mary had not done her homework. In supervision the therapist had been made aware of how she and Mary were polar opposites, with Mary acting passive and the therapist producing all the ideas and the action. The therapist therefore hit on the idea of asking Mary to use a flip chart and to go through the topic she had been asked to do as homework in the session. Mary showed no hesitation in doing this and quickly jumped up and took the marker pen. Mary wrote down several items.

Messages about the world I received as a child:

1. *Don't waste time playing, the xxs are at home studying.*
2. *There's no need to go outside the front gate. You have plenty within your own family to play with.*
3. *Others will try to hold you back.*
4. *The outside world is full of devious people.*
5. *xxs did brilliantly in their exams but this house is filled with numbskulls.*
6. *We are superior to many other people.*

The therapist and Mary linked this list with her present situation. Her social isolation was linked to messages 2, 3 and 4. The therapist also discussed the confusion in all the messages with 5 and 6 being mutually contradictory. The therapist was pleased that she had been cast less in the role of an advice-giver in this session and she felt optimistic that she had begun to make progress. The therapist was excited and amazed at how Mary had taken to this approach like a duck to water.

Mary was taking 18 laxative tablets a day and was vomiting just once a day. The therapist set more homework and asked Mary to write a letter to her mother describing her feelings about their relationship and also to write a letter to her bulimia as her friend.

(*Supervisor:* The use of the flip chart was an excellent concrete way to break out of the trap of active helpful therapist and passive patient. Mary was in the authoritative standing up position whereas the therapist put herself into a sitting down learning position. It is interesting that this session was followed, for the first time, by Mary doing a task for homework that had been set in the session. It is as if that, by breaking the ice, by doing a task within the session, the therapist had broken down the barrier between "homework" and work in the session. It is perhaps no wonder that Mary had balked at the thought of doing homework after having a mother who was also her teacher. Her rebellion is very understandable. On the other hand, her failure to fulfil the tasks may be related to her perfectionism or fear of failure or humiliation.)

Letter to my Mother
I can't pretend that it was my idea to write—it wasn't. It was that of my therapist. I don't quite know what I'm supposed to say, for I long since gave up trying to communicate anything other than gossip and banalities.

Remember the letter I wrote to you and Daddy when I left university? Why did you show it to everyone? Did you expect to provoke laughter and ridicule as you did with my letter to the radio when I was a child?

Our relationship has been a mess from the very beginning. I blame you because you were the adult and I was the child. I can understand your desire to produce a child prodigy, your interest in the theories of the educationalists of the time, but surely your common sense would have told you that by beating me and ridiculing me you were simply undermining my self-confidence and creating the opposite effect to the one you wished for.

Unfortunately, neither of us can undo the past. I suppose you did what you thought was best and I know that you did not have it easy.

But what annoys me now is that you do not seem to have learnt anything from the past. You still want to be in control. You still treat me like a child. Can't you understand that at nearly 40 it is intolerable to be told in your school mistress voice "No, you won't go into town"?

I would come home much more frequently if I thought it would be fun for all of us. It could be, but each time I find myself preparing for battle and each time I am obliged to assert my rights as an individual—different from you. Why can't you let go, accept me as I am, let me live, give me freedom?

(*Supervisor:* My first feeling was that Mary persists in taking on the passive role and tries to wriggle out of any active role. She states clearly at the beginning that the task is not hers but is her therapist's. I felt that it was impossible for her to construe, even in her imagination, a relationship with an equality of power.

A different way of looking at the letter is that Mary did express openly her ambivalence about writing it, which perhaps allowed her to then write about her relationship with her mother expressing her anger quite openly.

It is interesting that even in a more distant relationship with Mary, as a supervisor of her treatment, it is very easy to fall into the trap of feeling irritated and angry with her.)

Session 12

The therapist asked Mary to read the letter to bulimia nervosa as a friend. Mary had some difficulty in that she had made a small collection of notes. Once more the therapist invited Mary to use the flip chart. Mary wrote:

- *Being in control*
- *Acceptable*
- *Hard-working*
- *Dynamic-clever*
- *Sociable*
- *Energetic*

The therapist discussed with Mary in what other ways she could achieve these attributes without being thin. The therapist then discussed the negative aspects of bulimia nervosa.

(*Supervisor:* At last the therapist is focusing on Mary's ambivalence about change rather than, as it were, patting Mary to comfort her for the sadness she had met in her life.)

Sessions 13 and 14

Mary missed two sessions. She rang up to cancel one, saying that she had hurt her back. She became tearful and mentioned how upset she was about her therapist mentioning that time was running out in the last session.

Session 15

The therapist discussed the difficulty in getting a collaborative relationship if she continued to refuse to do her homework. Mary replied that she had been unable to put any active steps to change as many of them involved money. She was ashamed to tell her therapist that she spent all her money on food and so was unable to put any of the therapist's suggestions into practice. The therapist suggested that she was not ready to change. At the end of the session the therapist shocked herself by giving Mary a small hug. She felt very concerned about this afterwards and tried to rectify the balance in her summary letter at the end of treatment:

Dear Mary,

I did say when we were nearing the end of our last session that I would send you some details of a diet which you might find helpful. What we discussed still holds, which is that you need to concentrate on having three meals a day. And that these need to include, albeit not large, quantities of food that falls into the different categories: proteins—e.g. fish, chicken, meat, eggs; dairy products—e.g. cottage cheese, hard-soft cheeses, milk, yoghurt; vegetables—all kinds and as much variety as possible; cereals, bread and pasta products—e.g. especially Allbran, brown rice (especially), pasta, etc.; fruit—e.g. three times a day and even more if you feel like something sweet.

If that is not comprehensive enough you are more than welcome to make an appointment with our dietician.

Having said all that I think I need to stress that the more "psychological issues" are still the ones that would, in my view, be important ones to consider. We have discussed many of these over the weeks and months and I think by now you know that among these issues is the need for you to take control for yourself and to start making changes every week, little by little.

I hope you will consider this very seriously as we will need to decide on your next appointment whether you are ready at this stage to make these changes, or not.

I hope you have a good time at Christmas and that you will enjoy a happier and healthier New Year.

With kind regards,

(*Supervisor:* The therapist did not pick up on the missed sessions. They probably relate to Mary's ongoing difficulty in regulating closeness in the treatment. Mary then returns to the sessions as a tearful victim, with the therapist consoling her. Mary has thus successfully managed to get the therapist back into her old role of a rescuer, even to the extent of her trying to produce a magic diet sheet for Mary. It is unlikely that Mary doesn't know immensely more about nutrition than her therapist. The therapist in her letter avoids any emotional contact with Mary and keeps her at arms length. This reflects the massive shifts in emotional involvement that Mary induces.)

Addendum

After the Christmas break Mary came back for a meeting (Session 16) and she and her therapist reviewed progress. Mary was very keen on having more sessions and insisted that she wanted to work. Her therapist recanted and tried to work with Mary focusing on her ambivalence of working on her symptoms by giving more homework tasks. After a few sessions Mary's attendance again became erratic and her therapist and supervisor decided to put any therapy on hold. The therapist wrote to the referring doctor recommending that Mary be referred for therapy that focused on understanding her maladaptive cycles of behaviour and transference issues, such as cognitive analytical therapy.

This is the therapist's goodbye letter to Mary:

Dear Mary,

I have been impressed by the tenacity and the courage you showed in coming for treatment and even wanting to start again after Christmas. You have worked hard to show me a great deal about yourself and this has at times been very painful. You have exposed yourself to the risk of being criticised or let down—or worse, abused—all of which because of your past experiences, you are sensitised to.

Your bulimia acts as a shield to protect you from these forces and is a mechanism to block of the distress caused by loneliness, humiliation, resentment, etc. You are not even sure that you want a "NEW YOU".

You know from working with me that there is no magic bullet available. We have given you access to all that is known about the management of bulimia. What you need now is to be prepared to do it. This will require more work on the issues that keep you stuck, the patterns from the past and the distress that they cause. Such help is available and I have written to your general practitioner

CG74   CLINICIAN'S GUIDE

with suggestions. I wish you luck for the future and I know that you possess the inner resources to make the change.

Final Comment

With the wisdom of hindsight it is very easy to be critical of what went on in this therapy. Never once did the therapist address Mary's ambivalence. She never gave her a chance to make any self-motivating statements. Mary's passive resistance grew and grew until it collapsed into a mutual cycle of attack in the last session when Mary recognised that her next rescuer was going to leave her.

Mary prevented the therapist from working in a motivational way with her. The scene seemed to be set at the first session when Mary appeared so critical and rejecting, showing her new therapist the collection of scalps of earlier therapists.

This then led to a mutual cycle of pleasing behaviour. The therapist became very active, making suggestions for behavioural change and emphasising her therapeutic skills in making links between the past and the present. It was as if the therapist became totally determined to show what a good therapist she was. The therapist perceived Mary as a hurt, helpless and hopeless victim who needed rescuing and she would be able to do it if she were good enough. All her motivational skills flew out of the window. Even with supervision it was almost impossible to extricate the therapist from the rescuer trap.

What could have helped? The therapist should have allowed herself to listen and reflect more on Mary's ambivalence instead of frantically prescribing more and more homework tasks. It was as if filling in the homework sheets was the only way to tackle motivation. This certainly isn't the case. The exercises are merely a short cut and an *aide-mémoire*.

It may have helped if the therapist had done some homework herself and written a reformulation letter, early on, that emphasised the ambivalence and focused on the powerful interpersonal factors that were set into play.

In the first session the therapist should have seized upon Mary's open expression of ambivalence and poor motivation.

It is possible that instead of going through the tortuous route of 16 sessions plus several add-on sessions thereafter it might have been possible to point Mary earlier into the direction of a therapy that addressed her powerful schemata of thinking and maladaptive patterns of behaving, or to stop the sessions earlier (after an in-depth assessment with the offer to Mary to return at a later stage). However, people like Mary will perhaps always make us feel we are getting things wrong, which reflects her own powerful sense of failure.

This case has posed many questions and taught us many lessons:

- The therapist must be trained so that he or she has a good grasp of the spirit of motivational interviewing and doesn't just follow a rule book.
- Homework and structured tasks can be perceived by the client as being pushed into premature action or as a punishment. The therapist's aim is to try to raise the client's curiosity about issues that have been mentioned during the session and to wish to follow this up further. The resistance about not doing homework is as much a therapist problem as a client problem.
- It is possible to use motivational techniques on clients with powerful interpersonal schemata that easily trap the therapist. Good supervision is essential.

Workbook: Motivational Enhancement Therapy

WORKSHEET ONE:
TO CHANGE OR NOT TO CHANGE?

How motivated are you to change?

1	2	4	6	8	10

Not at all   Very

If you decided to change how confident are you that you would succeed?

1	2	4	6	8	10

Not at all   Very

How ready are you to change?

1	2	4	6	8	10

Not at all   Very

(Adapted from Rollnick et al., 1996)

WORKSHEET TWO: IS CHANGE REASONABLE?

How does the stranglehold of dieting and bulimia affect you? Think about your physical health, your psychological health, your social life, your family life, your romantic life, your education and career and your security.

Write a letter to the bulimia boa constrictor, your enemy.

WORKSHEET THREE: DIFFICULTIES OF CHANGE

What difficulties will you encounter when you start to struggle with your bulimia boa constrictor?

Write a letter to your bulimia boa constrictor as your friend.

WORKSHEET FOUR: FUTURE TIMES

How will you cope without your bulimia boa constrictor around you? Is it possible to imagine life without bulimia? What will have happened to your physical health, your psychological health, your family and social life and your career?

If you didn't have a bulimia boa constrictor around you who would you be? What do you really believe in? How do you want to live your life? If you had a magic wand what would you want to be? If you had to write a step by step computer program to achieve that magic goal, what would the steps be? Write down a list.

Write a letter to a friend five years in the future when you are free of your bulimia nervosa. Describe how your life in all its aspects will be changed.

Now write a letter to a friend five years in the future when you still have your bulimia nervosa.

WORKSHEET FIVE: PLANS FOR CHANGE

The changes I want to make are:

The most important reasons why I want to make these changes are:

The steps I plan to take in changing are:

The ways other people can help me are:

Person   Possible ways to help

I know that my plan is working if:

Some things that could interfere with my plan are:

(*Adapted from Miller et al., 1994*)

WORKSHEET SIX: WHAT SHOULD I WEIGH?

Height m (ft)	1.52 (5'0")	1.58 (5'2")	1.64 (5'4")	1.70 (5'6")	1.76 (5'8")
Normal Range	45–56kg 100–124lb 7–8½st	48–60kg 106–132lb 7½–9¼st	51–64kg 114–142lb 8–10st	54–68kg 119–150lb 8¼–10½st	58–72kg 136–160lb 9½–11¼st

(Normal Range: BMI 20–25)

My weight is _____

My height is _____

My BMI is _____
(BMI = weight in kilograms/height in metres squared)

My weight before bulimia nervosa began was _____

I have always been below average / average / above average weight
(*circle the correct one*)

My realistic target weight is _____

WORKSHEET SEVEN: WHAT DO I NEED TO EAT?

Age range (years)	Basal Metabolic Rate (BMR) (kcal/day)	Activity Level	
Women		**Women**	
10–18	12.2 x W + 746 = BMR	Inactive:	BMR x 1.30 = DEE
18–30	14.7 x W + 496 = BMR	Light:	BMR x 1.56 = DEE
30–60	8.7 x W + 829 = BMR	Moderate:	BMR x 1.64 = DEE
Men		**Men**	
10–18	17.5 x W + 651 = BMR	Inactive:	BMR x 1.30 = DEE
18–30	15.3 x W + 679 = BMR	Light:	BMR x 1.55 = DEE
30–60	11.6 x W + 879 = BMR	Moderate:	BMR x 1.78 = DEE

W = Weight in kg

DEE = Daily Energy Expenditure (kcal.day)

To estimate what you need to eat:

1. Put your weight in kilograms into the formula in the second column for your correct age and sex. This will give you your approximate basal metabolic rate (BMR).

> *Example: Woman, 27 years old, weight 59kg*
> $14.7 \times 59 + 496 = 1363$ (BMR)

My BMR is _____

2. Then put the BMR you have calculated into the formula against your activity level; this gives you your approximate daily energy expenditure (DEE)

> *Example: Woman, light activity level, BMR = 1363*
> $1363 \times 1.56 = 2126$ (DEE)

My DEE is _____

WORKSHEET EIGHT: STUCK IN THE DIETING PIT

How much "bulimic porn" do you read a week? (i.e. how many slimming magazines, cookery items, fashion books?) How does it make you feel?

Make a list of ways in which you could get more realistic images of women; e.g. visit art gallery, museum.

Which of these books have you read?

Fallon, P., Katzman, M.A., & Wooley, S.C. (1994). *Feminist perspectives on eating disorders*. New York: Guilford Press.

Ogdon, J. (1990). *Fat chance. The myth of dieting explained*. London: Routledge.

Omichinski, L., & Evans-Young, M. (1996). *You count, calories don't*. London: Hodder & Stoughton.

Sanders, T., & Bazalgette, P. (1993). *You don't have to diet*. London: Bantam Press.

Wolf, N. (1990). *The beauty myth*. London: Vintage.

WORKSHEET NINE:
THE WEB OF LIFE—INTERPERSONAL DIFFICULTIES

Some of the stresses and difficulties that make change difficult relate to other people.

Write your life story with an emphasis on important relationships in your life. Is there a pattern in your relationships? Do you keep running into the same sort of difficulty? Are you very shy? Is it difficult to trust others? Do you get let down frequently? Do you keep picking up frogs to see if you can transform them into princes?

Can you identify with any of these problems:

- Losing someone recently who was very important to you?
- Differences of opinion with someone who matters?
- Changes in the balance of relationships because of new roles; change of school, university, boyfriend?
- Split loyalties because of separations and divorces?

If the answer is yes then write about the bad and not so bad things about the relationship problem.

References

Bem, D.J. (1967). Self-perception: An alternative interpretation of cognitive dissonance phenomena. *Psychological Review, 74*, 183–200.

Chang, J. (1993). *Wild Swans*. Harmondsworth, UK: Penguin.

Fairburn, C.G., Norman, P.A., Welch, S.L., O'Connor, M.E., Doll, H.A., & Peveler, R.C. (1995). A prospective study of outcome in bulimia nervosa and long-term effects of three psychological treatments. *Archive of General Psychiatry, 52*, 304–312.

Greenberger, D., & Padesky, C.A. (1995). *Mind over mood*. New York: Guilford Press.

Linehan, M.M. (1993a). *Cognitive behavioural treatment of borderline personality disorders*. New York: Guilford Press

Linehan, M.M. (1993b). *Skills training manual for treating borderline personality disorder*. New York: Guilford Press.

Miller, W.R. (1983). Motivational interviewing with problem drinkers. *Behavioural Psychotherapy, 11*, 147–172.

Miller, W.R. (1995). *Motivational enhancement therapy with drug abusers*. (Personal communication)

Miller, W.R., & C'DeBaca, J. (1994). Quantum change: Toward a psychology of transformation. In T. Heatherton & J. Weinberger (Eds.), *Can personality change?* (pp.253–280). Washington, DC: American Psychological Association.

Miller, W.R. & Rollnick, S. (1991). *Motivational interviewing: Preparing people for change*. New York: Guilford Press.

Miller, W.R., & Sanchez, V.C. (1994). Motivating young adults for treatment and lifestyle change. In G. Howard (Ed.), *Issues in alcohol use and misuse by young adults* (pp.55–82). Notre Dame, IN: University Notre Dame Press.

Miller, W.R., Zweben, A., DiClementi, C.C., & Rychtarik, R.G. (1992). Motivational enhancement therapy manual: A clinical research guide for therapists treating individuals with alcohol abuse and dependence. National Institute on Alcohol Abuse and Alcoholism. *Project Match Monograph Series, Vol. 2*. (DHHS publication, ADFM 92 1994, Washington DC).

Padesky, C.A., & Greenberger, D. (1995). *Clinicians guide to mind over mood*. New York: Guilford Press.

Prochaska, J.O., & DiClemente, C.C. (1986). Towards a comprehensive model of change. In W.R. Miller & N. Heather (Eds.), *Treating addictive behaviours: Processes of change* (pp.3–27). New York: Plenum Press.

Prochaska, J.O., & DiClemente, C.C. (1992). Transtheoretical therapy. Toward a more integrative model of change. *Psychotherapy: Theory Research and Practice, 19*, 276–288.

Rogers, C.R. (1957). The necessary and sufficient conditions of therapeutic personality change. *Journal of Consulting Psychology, 21*, 95–103.

Rollnick, S., Kinnersley, P., & Stott, N. (1993). Methods of helping patients with behaviour change. *British Journal of Medicine, 307*, 188–190.

Rollnick, S., Mason, P., & Butler, C. (in prep). *Brief negotiation: A method for helping patients with behaviour change*.

Ryle, A. (1990). *Cognitive analytical therapy: Active participation in change*. Chichester: Wiley.

Sasson, J. (1993) *Princess: A true story of life behind the veil in Saudi Arabia*. UK: Avon Books

Young, J.E. (1990). *Cognitive therapy for personality disorders: A schema focused approach*. Sarasota, CA: Professional Resource Exchange.

GETTING BETTER
BIT(E) BY BIT(E)

The following pages comprise
the complete text of:

Getting Better Bit(e)
by Bit(e)

A Survival Kit for Sufferers of Bulimia
Nervosa and Binge Eating
Disorders

Ulrike Schmidt and Janet Treasure

Institute of Psychiatry
London, UK

Brunner-Routledge
Taylor & Francis Group

HOVE AND NEW YORK

Introduction

Although the media are now taking a great interest in eating disorders, perhaps this interest has served more to glamorise bulimic disorders than to inform about them. There still seems to be a great deal of mystique surrounding the problem, and there are many misconceptions and much misinformation about what causes bulimia, what the health risks are, and how the problem can be overcome. Access to treatment is still very difficult for sufferers living in many parts of the country, and their friends and relatives often feel completely in the dark as to what to do to help. Some doctors are not very sympathetic to sufferers, enhancing their sense of guilt and loneliness.

This book was originally written for the bulimic patients attending the Eating Disorder Clinic at the Maudsley Hospital. Many of the patients we see need basic information about the various aspects of their difficulty and simple practical advice on how to overcome the problem. The psychotherapy programmes run by our unit and by other eating disorder clinics in this country attempt to address these issues. This book contains in condensed form what we know to be the essential ingredients of treatment. The book has now been given to a large number of eating disorder patients attending our clinic, and we have been very encouraged by their response. Many of them, upon reading it, felt empowered to tackle their eating problem and, beyond that, to address other difficulties in their lives too. Other patients—often those who were less sure about what they wanted—felt that the book did help them to understand their problems better and has given them the tools to make an informed decision about whether or not to enter treatment.

This book could help you, too, to make the journey to recovery and act as your guide. You must undertake the journey of change yourself, but we hope to provide maps and to point out the dangers and pitfalls along the route.

You may have mixed feelings about leaving the security of the familiar territory of bulimia nervosa. Although you know that there are severe dangers on all sides, you may have constructed a smoke screen which keeps the dangers out of sight. You will be frightened about entering the new territory where there may be no comfort or protection. This book is filled with the travellers' tales of people like yourself who have made the journey before you. Many of our patients have contributed to this book. We have recorded their stories and their suffering to help decrease your sense of isolation.

This book will help you avoid the snares that self-defeating thought patterns will throw up to catch you. It contains the tools needed to make the journey and travel along the road to recovery. It will show you changes that you can make so that the short-lived rewards that you get from bulimia are replaced by better, more long-lasting alternatives.

With this book you should be able to anticipate, and be prepared for, holdups and detours on the way. You may have some initial discomfort (for example, any new exercise will produce transient aches as new muscle groups are brought into use), but eventually you will recognise the benefits of your new-found strengths.

Not everyone is able to make the trip successfully the first time. Setbacks and relapses commonly occur. However, you will be able to learn from your setbacks and relapses. For some sufferers, the change process is slow and laborious, and it takes many attempts before the goal is attained; others will find that the way is easier.

People differ in how long the journey to recovery should take. Three months is the average, but it is often necessary to consult the maps or guides at intervals over a few years to ensure that strong currents have not returned you to bulimia nervosa once more.

You may feel "I can't help myself. I have tried. My problem is too severe for this. I need someone else to take over." Any form of treatment can only work if you are actively involved. The more you put in, the more you will get out of it. So you might as well make a start now. However, we don't expect that anything that you read in this book will suddenly make you "snap out of your problem". By making a decision to stop your chaotic eating pattern, you will have taken the important first step on a journey that leads to increased freedom and increased self-esteem.

A FEW WORDS OF CAUTION

A number of people are persuaded by their families or partners to work on their problems. This book can only help you if YOU really want to get better for YOURSELF. It can't help if you are not ready to change, or if you just want to change for somebody else's sake. To assess this you need to go to chapter 1 and fill in your own balance sheet and then keep it with you (in your bag or pocket) for regular consultation wherever you go.

You will be asked to embark on a lot of hard work over the next few weeks. Even if you are very determined to get better, there are bound to be ups and downs. The best way to deal with this is to take each day as it comes and not to dwell on the past.

You may feel a temptation to "binge" on this book, i.e. to read it quickly and to throw it into a corner, and tell yourself you knew it all already. If you are honest to yourself, that is probably not true. Try to digest each chapter slowly.

WHAT THIS BOOK CAN AND CAN'T DO

This book can't cure you. However, the book can help you to get much better, so that the eating disorder doesn't rule your life any more. The book is not aimed primarily at helping you to understand why you developed an eating problem. Understanding the underlying causes is often difficult and only happens very gradually; in some cases it may be impossible. Although understanding what caused the eating problem is important, it does not often in itself help to change distressing eating symptoms. This book is aimed at helping people to improve their symptoms and to gain some control over their lives. Once eating symptoms have improved, the underlying causes often become a lot clearer, and it is much more possible to decide then whether they need treatment in their own right.

FURTHER READING

Abraham, S., & Llewellyn-Jones, D. (1992). *Eating disorders—The facts*. Oxford: Oxford Medical Publications.

Buckroyd, J. (1989). *Eating your heart out. The emotional meaning of eating disorders*. London: MacDonald Optima.

Dana, M., & Lawrence, M. (1989). *Women's secret disorder. A new understanding of bulimia*. London: Grafton Books.

Duker, M., & Slade, R. (1990). *Anorexia and bulimia—How to help*. Milton Keynes: Open University Press.

French, B. (1987). *Coping with bulimia. The binge-purge syndrome*. Wellingborough: Thorsons Publishing Group.

Hollis, J. (1985). *Fat is a family affair. A guide for people with eating disorders and those who love them.* Center City, MN: Hazelden.

Lawrence, M. (ed.) (1987). *Fed Up and Hungry.* London: Women's Press.

Melville, J. (1983). *The ABC of eating. Coping with anorexia, bulimia and compulsive eating.* London: Sheldon Press.

Orbach, S. (1978). *Fat is a feminist issue.* London: Hamlyn Paperbacks.

Orbach, S. (1984). *Fat is a feminist issue 2.* London: Hamlyn Paperbacks.

Roche, L. (1984). *Glutton for punishment. A personal story of the bingeing/starving syndrome.* London: Pan Books.

Singh, J., & Rosier, P. (1990). *No body's perfect. Dealing with food problems.* Dublin: Attic Handbooks.

CHAPTER ONE

The Way Forward

DO I SUFFER FROM BULIMIA?

There is a bewildering number of labels that acknowledge that a person has a problem with overeating and is distressed about it. You may have come across some of them: compulsive overeating, bulimia nervosa, bulimia, binge eating disorder, or bulimarexia. These labels overlap and have an awful lot in common with each other. Problems with overeating can occur in people of any body weight (skinny, average, and overweight). This book has been written for people who fall into any of these categories. If you are unsure whether any of this fits you, fill in and score the test in Table 1.1.

If your severity index score is 5 points or above, it is very likely that you have a significant eating disorder at present.

If your symptom score is 15 points or above, you have a lot of the thoughts and attitudes that go with an eating disorder and are clearly distressed by it.

HOW TO USE THIS BOOK

Like many people, you may have the habit of starting books at the end or in the middle, perhaps flicking through the pages and beginning with a chapter with a particularly catching title. In principle there is nothing to stop you doing that with this book, but there are a few things that you need to know before you make a start: Chapters 1 to 6 are the core

TABLE 1.1
Bulimic Investigatory Test, Edinburgh

Questions	Scores
1. Do you have a regular daily eating pattern? Yes = 0, No = 1	___
2. Are you a strict dieter? Yes = 1, No = 0	___
3. Do you feel a failure if you break your diet once? Yes = 1, No = 0	___
4. Do you count the calories of everything you eat, even when not on a diet? Yes = 1, No = 0	___
5. Do you ever fast for a whole day? Yes = 1, No = 0	___
6. If yes, how often is this? Have once = 1; now and then = 2; once a week = 3; 2–3 times a week = 4; every second day = 5	___
7. Do you do any of the following to help you lose weight? (a) Take diet pills; (b) Take diuretics (water tablets); (c) Take laxatives; (d) Make yourself vomit. Never = 0; occasionally = 2; once a week = 3; 2–3 times a week = 4; daily = 5; 2–3 times a day = 6; 5+ times a day = 7. Answer questions 7 (a)–(d) separately, then add them all up.	___
8. Does you pattern of eating severely disrupt your life? Yes = 1, No = 0	___
9. Would you say that food dominated your life? Yes = 1, No = 0	___
10. Do you ever eat and eat until you are stopped by physical discomfort? Yes = 1, No = 0	___
11. Are there times when all you think about is food? Yes = 1, No = 0	___
12. Do you eat sensibly in front of others and make up in private? Yes = 1, No = 0	___
13. Can you always stop eating when you want to? Yes = 0, No = 1	___
14. Do you experience overpowering urges to eat and eat and eat? Yes = 1, No = 0	___
15. When you are feeling anxious do you tend to eat a lot? Yes = 1, No = 0	___
16. Does the thought of becoming fat terrify you? Yes = 1, No = 0	___
17. Do you ever eat large amounts of food rapidly (not a meal)? Yes = 1, No = 0	___
18. Are you ashamed of your eating habits? Yes = 1, No = 0	___
19. Do you worry that you have no control over how much you eat? Yes = 1, No = 0	___
20. Do you turn to food for comfort? Yes = 1, No = 0	___

(Continued)

TABLE 1.1 *(Continued)*
Bulimic Investigatory Test, Edinburgh

Questions	Scores
21. Are you able to leave food on the plate at the end of a meal? Yes = 0, No = 1	___
22. Do you deceive other people about how much you eat? Yes = 1, No = 0	___
23. Does how hungry you feel determine how much you eat? Yes = 0, No = 1	___
24. Do you ever binge on large amounts of food? Yes = 1, No = 0	___
25. If yes, do such binges leave you feeling miserable? Yes = 1, No = 0	___
26. If you do binge, is this only when you are alone? Yes = 1, No = 0	___
27. If you do binge, how often is this? Hardly ever = 1; once a month = 2; once a week = 3; 2–3 times a week = 4; daily = 5; 2–3 times a day = 6	___
28. Would you go to great lengths to satisfy an urge to binge? Yes = 1, No = 0	___
29. If you overeat do you feel very guilty? Yes = 1, No = 0	___
30. Do you ever eat in secret? Yes = 1, No = 0	___
31. Are your eating habits what you would consider to be normal? Yes = 0, No = 1	___
32. Would you consider yourself to be a compulsive eater? Yes = 1, No = 0	___
33. Does your weight fluctuate by more than 5 pounds in a week? Yes = 1, No = 0	___
Adding up and analysing the scores	
Total for questions 6, 7 and 27. This will give you a severity index.	___
Total for all other questions. This will give you a symptom score.	___

Adapted from M. Henderson & C.P.L. Freeman (1987). *British Journal of Psychiatry,* *150,* 18–24. Reproduced with permission.

chapters that will teach you all the steps you need for cracking unhealthy eating habits. It is sensible to read chapters 1 to 6 together, but you can do this in whatever order you like. With the help of these chapters you will be able to decide whether you are correct in making the decision that you want to get over your bulimia and are ready to do so.

If in addition to a problem with your eating habits you are also overweight, you should include chapter 7 in your initial reading.

Chapters 8 to 14 focus on the links between your eating disorder and the rest of your life. You can read them at a leisurely pace over the next few weeks, in whatever order you like. The aim of these additional chapters is to help you spot problems in different areas of your life, to get you to make some connections with factors that may have contributed to the origins of your eating problem or are obstacles for overcoming it.

If you are currently drinking heavily or are regularly taking drugs, you should look at chapter 12 early on. Drug and alcohol problems make your eating difficulty much more difficult to control and should therefore be tackled early on. Chapter 12 will help you (a) to assess how serious your alcohol/drug problem is, and (b) to decide what to do about it.

FIRST STEPS

Are You Ready to Undertake the Journey?

Before starting, it is important to dip into the core chapters (2–6) of the book to obtain basic background information.

Read chapters 2, 3, 4, 5, & 6 Now. Don't attempt to follow any of the instructions given there, skip over these. Re-read each chapter until you are sure that you have been able to take the information on board. Are you ready to undertake the journey?

• Now, when you have a quiet hour, work on writing your bulimia balance sheet.

First, take a large sheet of paper and divide it length-wise into two main columns. At the top of one column write, "Reasons for giving up bulimia", and on the other write, "Reasons for staying bulimic". You may have important reasons to fear change from familiar behaviour, and yet part of you is desperate to shake yourself out of the vicious circle that is keeping your bulimia nervosa going. It is impossible to keep all these thoughts and ideas together in your head at one time as our memory has its limits, and so there is a tendency to swing from one side of an argument to the other. Writing a balance sheet will help you to deal with all of your thoughts systematically. Plan to work on this project during a week—keep going back to it each day.

In order to focus your thoughts, make four divisions across the sheet and at the start of each row, write:

1. Practical gains and losses for SELF
2. Practical gains and losses for OTHERS
3. Emotional gains and losses for SELF (self-approval or self-disapproval)
4. Emotional gains and losses for OTHERS (social approval or disapproval)

Here are examples from the balance sheets of others, which may help to get you started. You may agree with some of the comments and want to add them to your list. But give yourself time to find your own reasons, and make them as specific as possible. Have this balance sheet in the back of your mind all week, so that new ideas can pop up unexpectedly when you are doing something else.

Reasons to Give up Bulimia
1. *Practical gains to self*
    "I won't be tired and unwell all the time."
    "My teeth won't continue to be destroyed."
    "I will look healthier."
    "My guts will work normally without unnatural practices."
    "My body will begin to repair the damage I have caused."
2. *Practical gains for others*
    "I will be able to spend more time with my family and friends and will not have to make excuses to avoid eating with them."
    "My flatmates won't find the food cupboards empty."
    "I will be more romantically/sexually responsive."
    "My partner will be able to kiss me if I no longer vomit."
    "I will be less irritable and snappy."
    "I will be able to concentrate and do a better job at work."
3. *Self-approval*
    "I won't have to lie about food and how much I eat."
    "I won't have to deceive people about vomiting and taking laxatives."
    "I will have achieved something positive."
4. *Social approval*
    "My parents will stop worrying that I will die."
    "My friends won't have to see me destroying my life."
    "My parents/husband/boyfriend will no longer have to suffer the shame of being associated with someone suffering from an obvious psychiatric disorder."
    "At work I will appear healthy and competent."
    "I will be able to join in all social activities without excuses."

Disadvantages of Change and Recovery
1. *Practical loss to self*
    "I will find meal-times very frightening."
    "I will feel bloated and stuffed too full."
    "My stomach may 'blow out' after eating small amounts."
    "I may get some swelling around my eyes and ankles."
    "I will become very frightened about my weight."
2. *Practical loss to others*
    "I will need more active help and support from my parents/spouse."
    "My mood may swing more."

3. *Self-disapproval*
   "It will be so difficult that I'm bound to fail and then I will feel worse than ever."
   "I will feel out of control over everything."
   "I will have to face up to my responsibilities."
   "I will feel uncomfortable, miserable, and frightened."
   "I will hate myself and my body."
4. *Social disapproval*
   "I will no longer be able to let others think that I am controlled about eating and my weight."
   "I may become more assertive and dominant when relieved of this burden of shame and guilt, which may upset the status quo in my relationships."

Don't worry if you find it difficult to distinguish between these four categories, which have just been made to help focus your thoughts. There is quite a bit of overlap between them. It doesn't really matter which exact category you put any reason in, as long as it is in the correct column, i.e. positive or negative.

When your balance sheet is finished, go over the list and give each reason a rating on a 1–10 scale (10 = a very important reason; 1 = only slightly important reason).

BACK TO THE FUTURE

We now suggest that you do the following exercise. You will find it helpful to have your balance sheet in front of you while you do it.

Imagine yourself in five years' time, after you had decided that it was too difficult and risky to overcome your eating disorder. You continue to have bulimia nervosa. Everything has gone wrong. All the negative consequences that you considered in your balance sheet have come true. You feel at the end of your tether. You decide to write to your one close friend, whom you haven't seen for a while as she (assuming your friend is a woman) has been abroad. You know that she cares about you and will not be deceived by superficial news and that when you meet her on her return she will see it all anyway. You have found in the past that she has been able to provide emotional and practical support when you have needed help. You know that you can, and must, give her a full account of your present difficulties.

Here Are a Few Guidelines for You to Consider.
- What weight will you be?
- What medical complications will you have?
- What career/job will you be pursuing?

- Where and with whom will you be living?
- Who will be your friends?
- Will you be in a relationship? married? have children?

Now be as realistic as possible, and talk in the present tense. Here is an example of a letter from another sufferer from bulimia nervosa, who is preparing herself to undertake the journey of recovery:

25th May 1998

Dear Susan,

I am looking forward to seeing you again in June. I thought I should be open with you about my current situation so that we can pick up where we left off when you arrive back. I'm afraid it's rather a sad story, but I know I can trust you with it, and I even have faith that something good will come out of it, as happened in the past.

My bulimia has continued, which means I have had it for 15 years now. My weight has fluctuated greatly between 8 and 13 stone. At the moment I am just over 8 stone, but I remain unhappy.

I continue to vomit, although it doesn't seem to be as effective as it once did, and I now severely restrict my food. I spend all day preparing my food. I keep a semblance of control by wrapping small bites in dried seaweed. In the morning I sometimes wake to find that I have eaten at night but cannot remember it. The illness has taken a severe toll on my health. I now have six caps on my teeth, and the others remain very sensitive to temperature changes. Last summer I was in hospital in agonizing pain with kidney stones. I had special new vibration treatment to disperse them. I passed blood and gravel in my urine for weeks afterwards.

I'm more hooked on laxatives than ever before. I spend all day walking to chemists' shops to buy them. I have a fixed routine and visit different shops on different days of the week. I spend more than half my social security money on laxatives. I have found that the amount I need gradually increases. Without laxatives I become so bloated and bunged up that I am terrified, and yet with them I bleed and leak and am up all night on the toilet.

I have not worked for the past two years. I rent a room in a house with six others. Since David finished with me four years ago, my social life has shrunk. I only remain in contact with Sophie and Paul. They write to me regularly and come and pick me up to take me to their house. At times I feel so low and so full of despair that I contemplate ending my suffering. I hold back as I am a coward and also because I couldn't bear to think of people seeing my room or belongings after I am dead. I would be ashamed for them to see my hoards of food (I have 3 deep freezers filled with food) and my hoard of trinkets, which I have stolen from shops and never used. The compulsion to collect and clean is overwhelming.

Despite all of this, I do have a glimmer of hope. I remember that five years ago you offered to help me overcome my illness. It seemed too difficult and risky then to change. However, I now see that there is no other way forward, and I would like to accept that offer of help that you so generously made before.

I know that you will be pleased that I have made this first step and have written to you.

With love from Penny

- Now write your own letter. Read it through very carefully. Do you really want a future like this?
- Refer back to the guidelines at the start of this section. Now write a second letter. Imagine your situation in five years. This time you have successfully controlled your bulimia. Is this the sort of future you want to aim for?

MAKING YOUR DECISION TO GO

Whether you decide now to work at change or to continue with bulimia nervosa will result from a decision made by you. It will probably not be simply a question of one decision but of numerous smaller decisions that you will make over the following days, months, and years. There will be strong forces sucking you back. You will make many mistakes; after all, you are human and fallible. However, being human, you can also learn from your mistakes.

Should I Involve Someone to Help Me?

Trying to get better on your own is a hard and a lonely task. In some cases it is useful to enlist the help of family or friends. Sometimes your family may be keener on the idea of helping you than you are to have them help you. If you are unsure whether to involve your family or friends, you should look at chapter 13, which will help you clarify whether it might be a positive step for you to involve them in your treatment, how to involve them in the best way, and whether you are asking them for the right reasons. You will need to decide whom you will ask to give you support. Will it be people you are closest to or those that you spend most time with?

The questions outlined in Table 1.2 may help you in making a decision.

TABLE 1.2

Support Questionnaire

Could person X be your support? Answer the following questions:	Score
1. How easy is it to talk to X about your problem? Very easy (5 points); quite easy (4 points); Not sure (3 points); quite difficult (2 points); very difficult (1 point)	——
2. Is X critical or easily upset about your eating? Always (1 point); often (2 points); sometimes (3 points); rarely (4 points); never (5 points)	——
3. Could you talk to X even if you weren't making progress? Definitely (3 points); not sure (2 points); definitely not (1 point)	——
4. Can you trust X to be always there when you need someone—with no strings attached? Definitely (5 points); probably (4 points); maybe (3 points); probably not (2 points); definitely not (1 point)	——
5. If you overcame your bulimia, what would X's likely response be? (a) X would feel quite threatened by this and feel redundant (0 points) (b) X would feel jealous of me becoming more independent and successful with my life (0 points) (b) I haven't a clue (1 point) (b) X would be very pleased for me (2 points)	——
6. How often are you in contact with X? At least once a week (3 points) At least once every fortnight (2 points) At least once a month (1 point) Less than once a month (0 points)	——
Total number of points	——

Analysing your score

19 to 23 points: You are in the lucky position of having a perfect supporter near you. You should definitely ask person X to help you in your efforts to overcome your eating disorder.

12 to 18 points: It is uncertain whether X should be your supporter. Maybe you don't know them well enough yet to be able to say what their response to you would be. Perhaps your best bet is to keep X in mind as a potential support, but not to rush into anything. However, if you do know X very well, your score may simply reflect that X is rather luke-warm about their commitment to you, and you may be better off thinking about someone else.

4 to 11 points: Look for someone else, or go it alone.

Asking for support will be difficult. Try to be as direct and as specific about what you want your potential supporter to do as possible. Perhaps you should give them this book to look at.

Helping someone with an eating problem is a difficult task. Some people may foresee these problems and decline to help early on. You should expect this. It is not rejection but realism. Others may take it on, wishing to please and help you without knowledge of the implications and then find it too difficult—you should expect this. Again, it is not rejection but realism.

If you are lucky, you may have one of those rare people around you, who will be able to help and stick with it. It will be difficult and treacherous for both of you, but the rewards are great. You will need to take an active part in defining the amount of support that will be helpful. Spend at least 15 minutes per week reviewing progress and setting new goals with your "co-therapist". You may want to show or share with your "co-therapist" some of the exercises we suggest in this book.

Trust will be a difficult issue. The secret life of a sufferer with an eating disorder leads to suspiciousness in others. You will need to discuss this with your supporter. Tell them that if they become suspicious or anxious, they should talk to you about it. Encourage them to state what has made them worried. They must try to be direct and present the facts, rather than carry out a character assassination or withdraw their help with "the hump". For example, they may need to say, "You've been working hard not to binge, and you have been able to join with me for several evenings. However, you ate very little at supper last night and appeared tense and rushed off so early. I'm wondering if you've started to binge and vomit again."

You may work with your supporter to think of ways to alter your behaviour when you get an urge to eat. For example, you may come home from a difficult day at work feeling tense and hopeless, with thoughts such as "I never do anything right" spinning in your head. Instead of bingeing, which would temporarily remove these thoughts, you may try to go out for a walk with your supporter to discuss together your thoughts and feelings and gain a different perspective.

An alternative form of support that may work for you might be to join the self-help meetings run by the Eating Disorders Association (address at the end of the book). Parents or concerned others often find these meetings helpful too, and can feel that they are doing something useful and yet are less intrusive.

Even if you decide to go it alone, it will be a good idea to set aside 30 minutes each week (or more frequently) for review. Try to use your diary as a friend and confidante. Perhaps use this time to write a letter as if to a "co-therapist", or paint yourself a picture or a collage summarising the week. End by marking goals into your diary for this week and evaluating progress of difficulties from the week before.

HOW TO STAGE YOUR JOURNEY

Before you begin to work with this book (after you have browsed through it and done the introductory exercises), you must decide—perhaps with the help of your supporter—to set yourself realistic and manageable goals. It will be very overwhelming to state: "I am never going to binge again in my life." Such an over-keen, unrealistic goal can be a trigger for more binges! It helps if you break down your overall goals into more manageable steps. Chapters 2 to 6 will help you to get some idea of what goals might be realistic as starting points in order to overcome various aspects of your eating disorder. In trying to reach a goal, it is important to have an exact description of what you want. This must be in terms of:

1. Something that you can plan and do yourself.
2. It must be something that is measurable (not just something that is impossible to measure, such as happiness).
3. Goals should challenge you slightly, so that you will feel pleased when they are done, but not so impossible that only Wonder-woman alone could accomplish them.
4. Goals should be defined within a realistic time frame. Having no time limit leads to procrastination. Having a goal in which you state: "I will not do X for the rest of my life" is equally unhelpful, as you would only know that you had met your goal when you were dead.

Think of The Little Engine and The Hill. This small engine was able to conquer the hill by saying:

"I think I can, I'm sure I can,
I think I can, I'm sure I can".

CHAPTER TWO

Tools for the Journey

HOW TO KEEP A THERAPEUTIC DIARY

Have a look at the sample diary page at the back of this book. If you have access to a photocopier, why not just copy it? You can then carry a single diary sheet around with you every day, and collect all the sheets in a folder. If you don't have access to a photocopier, you will have to make up your own diary. Buy a booklet small enough to fit into your pockets or a bag. The ground rules for keeping a diary are simple:

- The diary is to help you as a friend would. It is not meant to be a persecuting "spy in the cab".
- For every day, write down what you have eaten and drunk. Try to be as accurate as you can.
- Write down those occasions when you should have eaten or drunk but avoided it.
- Always keep your diary with you. Take it with you even to the loo. Record even things you find shameful and embarrassing.
- Record things when they are happening. That gives the clearest idea of what was going on at the time.
- Do not write a novel: try to find a "short-hand" way of describing what was happening at the time.
- Do not leave writing your diary till the end of the day, as this will make it very inaccurate.

Until you get into the habit of diary-keeping, you may want to break it down into stages. Get used to scribbling down what you eat for a week or two; thereafter move on to the ABC approach described below. The detective work then follows.

"A" is for antecedents (triggers). Write down:

- Where were you at the time of eating, and what was going on (i.e. were you on your own or in company, at home or at work, etc.)?
- What were your thoughts beforehand? Who said what?
- What were your feelings beforehand?

"B" is for behaviour. Write down:

- Whether you thought what you ate was a binge.
- Whether you were sick and how often.
- Whether you used laxatives or diuretics, and in what amounts.

"C" is for consequences. Write down:

- What were the consequences—both positive and negative—in both the short and long term upon your thoughts, feelings, and behaviour?

You can then build up the behaviour chain:

	thoughts			positive consequences
"A"		→ "B" Behaviour → "C"		
	feelings			negative consequences

The most difficult aspect of the detective work will be to become aware of your triggering thoughts and feelings. Chapter 10, "Food for Thought", describes the thinking traps that commonly occur with eating disorders. Most triggering thoughts and feelings are unpleasant, and you may prefer not to dwell on them, but the energy used to blot them out takes a long-term toll on well-being. Although these thoughts and feelings are not enjoyable, they are necessary and important signals that indicate that you may need to change some aspects of your life. In Table 2.1 we have included excerpts from a diary sheet completed by Anna, one of our patients, as an example.

Although this diary should only take a few minutes a day to complete, you are bound to find keeping it on a daily basis inconvenient at times, if not irritating. Start it on a day when you are not so busy that you are bound to fail to keep it. Keeping it for one or two days a week completely is better than one week of inaccuracies.

TABLE 2.1
Anna's Food Diary, Week 1 and Week 4

Week 1

Time	What eaten	B	V	L	Antecedents & Consequences
8.00	All-bran				A: Still full from yesterday. C: Must make an effort not to binge today.
12.00	1 apple				A: Hungry. C: Still hungry, mustn't eat more in case it starts me off on a binge.
3.00	1lb grapes, 2 choc. bars		!		A: Had phone call from John, he would be home late. C: Disgusted with myself. I am the most hopeless person in the world.
6.00	peanuts & chocolates, picked from shopping	!!			A: No food in flat. Had to go shopping. Couldn't stop myself putting loads of sweets in the trolley. Ate loads of stuff in the car. Had to go on eating once at home.
			!!		
7.00	2 portions of curry, 3 choc. bars	!!	!!		C: Very angry with myself. I feel so lonely. Totally exhausted, went to bed early.

Week 4

Time	What eaten	B	V	L	Antecedents & Consequences
8.00	Cottage cheese,2 sl. toast with honey				Enjoyed this.
11.00	apple				
12.30	baked potato, tuna fish				Eaten in the canteen at work. Tina said: "You haven't been here for ages." Could have run away, felt everybody was looking at me.
3.00	yoghurt, crunch bar				
6.00	1 sl. of toast				
7.00	fish & vegetables, 1 portion of ice cream				Had not planned dessert. John suggested ice cream. My initial response was to say no, but I knew I would then finish the packet off whilst washing up. So I had a portion and enjoyed it sitting with John. John put it away and made coffee, which we drank relaxing on the settee. Washing up left.

B = Binge, V = Vomited, L = Laxatives

We find that people vary greatly in their response to keeping this diary. You may be a person who loves writing diaries and who is able to treat it like a trusted, reliable friend in whom you have no difficulty confiding. Good. You will not have any difficulties with the approach used.

On the other hand, for a variety of reasons you may absolutely loathe keeping a diary. You may simply find it boring. Or you may find it very frightening and shameful and find it extremely hard to face up to what you are doing to yourself. You may also be worried about someone else finding the diary. Or perhaps you worry that it might make you worse to concentrate on your food intake so much. You may feel very tempted to stop writing your diary every time you have had a binge. Try to be as honest as you can. It must be said that getting over this problem will involve facing up to very frightening feelings, thoughts, and behaviour. Blocking these off will not help in the long term.

Some people find that simply keeping a diary helps them to regularise their eating habits and may lead to considerable improvement. For others it may not be that easy.

Shula

Shula had severe anorexia nervosa. She spent a long time in hospital, and her weight increased to the level it had been before the onset of her illness. However, after discharge she was left with very painful, prolonged binges, which happened every day. She induced vomiting several times a day and took about 150 laxative pills a day. She kept her food diary religiously, as she felt it gave her some sense of being in control amidst all her chaos. After three or four months of keeping a diary (and trying to work on her eating problem), she felt that very little had changed, so why continue keeping it? Shula was asked to go over her diary again and to draw up a chart of the number of binges, episodes of vomiting, and number of laxatives taken per week (Figure 2.1).

To her surprise, she discovered that she had actually decreased all the features of her eating problem, most remarkably the laxatives, but that bingeing and vomiting were also reducing gradually. You may say, "How could she have failed to notice such a dramatic improvement?" Well, it's very easy when change is drawn out over a long period of time, and especially on a bad day, when everything looks gloomy to you. Shula decided to put up the weekly chart in her bedroom, to give her strength at times when she felt she wasn't changing.

No. of tablets
per week

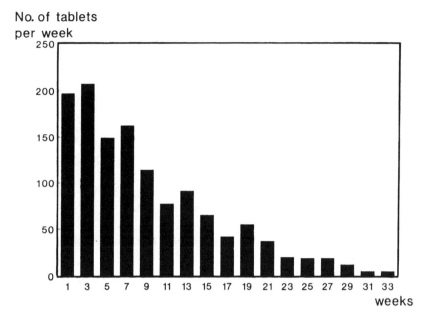

weeks

FIG. 2.1. Laxative chart.

NEW SKILLS TO COPE WITH OLD DIFFICULTIES

You will find that, in gradually learning to give up retreating into the patterns of bulimia nervosa as a means of coping with life's difficulties, you will need to develop new skills.

Learning to Solve Problems in Seven Steps

Making decisions and solving problems, small or large, is a definite skill. People vary in the ways they reach solutions for problems. Some do it just intuitively; it has to feel right emotionally or agree with certain "rules" that they live by. Others do it mainly by trying to find the most rational solution. There is no right or wrong way and we all use mixtures of these two approaches. The seven steps outlined below are guidelines which are useful to follow when you are trying to find a way of coping with life's demands and stresses without bulimia nervosa.

Step 1: What is the problem? This step may sound trivial, but you do need to define your problem carefully. Try to write one simple sentence putting your problem in a nutshell.

Step 2: Finding possible solutions. Many people get stuck because in trying to find a solution they limit themselves too early in the number of alternative solutions they consider. Put all constraints aside and try to find as many solutions as you can. Let your imagination run riot. Do not exclude anything just because it seems selfish, crazy, unrealistic, or far fetched. Jot down anything that comes into your mind.

Step 3: Looking at options in detail. For each solution you have found go through the pros and cons, even for those solutions that seem silly.

Step 4: Choosing a solution that fits you. By going through step 3 you should have a clearer sense of what is right or wrong for you. If you are still unsure what seems to be the best option, you may have to go back to step 2 and create more solutions, or you may not be ready to do anything about the problem you have defined. Can it be shelved for a while? What are the pros and cons of doing that?

Step 5: Finding ways of putting your solution into practice. Think through all the steps needed to reach your solution.

Step 6: Carry it out step by step.

Step 7: Check the final outcome to ensure that your solution has been a suitable one.

In chapter 1 we showed you how to use the first steps of problem solving to make the decision to get over your bulimia nervosa. You may want to read over your bulimia nervosa balance sheet now. In chapter 14 we discuss the use of problem solving in relation to career decisions. Here is an example which applies problem solving to relationships:

Andrea

Andrea's boyfriend, Ian, had recently split up with her. Shortly afterwards, Phil, one of her old boyfriends, began to ring her up daily and to visit her regularly. Her parents, who had greatly disliked Ian, supported this development. Her mother would repeatedly tell her how nice Phil was, and she would invite him round to their house without telling Andrea. Andrea was confused and upset about splitting up with Ian, she was angry about her mother's attempts to pair her off with Phil, and she was irritated, but also flattered, by Phil's attention. She felt that the pressure she was put under, both by her mother and by Phil, to go out with him was hard to resist and that she might end up giving in to it. After having been told about the problem-solving approach, Andrea defined her problem in terms of the seven steps:

Step 1: My problem is, I don't know what I want. Part of me knows I am not ready to enter a new relationship and that I need space and time to get over Ian, who hurt me really badly. Part of me feels that if my mother, whose judgement I trust in other things, approves of Phil, he must be good for me. And also, as he clearly cares so much about me, maybe I'd be a fool to reject him.

Steps 2 and 3: Andrea then wrote down the following possible solutions:

(a) To become Phil's girlfriend again. Pros: This would keep everyone happy, my feeling of being under pressure would ease, I would have someone to comfort me. Cons: In the long run I'd probably feel as discontented and bored as when I went out with Phil before.

(b) Never to see Phil again and put the phone down every time he rings. Pros: It would give me space and ease pressure. Cons: I would definitely lose a good friend.

(c) To avoid going home to see my parents till they have accepted that I don't want to be with Phil. Pros: Again, pressure would be reduced. Cons: I would miss my parents, I like going home, and I appreciate my mother's advice on most issues.

(d) To beg Ian to make a fresh start. Pros: If he took me back, I'd be unbelievably happy. Cons: If he said no to me, I'd feel even more hurt than I do now.

(e) To find myself another boyfriend. Pros: It would be like making a completely new start. Cons: Nice new boyfriends aren't all that easy to find. Moreover, at the moment I don't think I can feel anything for a new person.

(f) To run away to the South Pacific. Pros: I'd be away from all the misery, and all the new impressions would help me to get over my upset. Cons: I don't have the money. Travelling can be a lonely affair, especially when you are not feeling your best.

(g) To take an overdose and risk dying. Pros: It would make Ian realise how much he hurt me. Although it would probably not make him change his mind about finishing with me, I would have the grim satisfaction of knowing I had got back at him. It would really teach him a lesson. Cons: I am really scared of dying. I might seriously damage my health and end up as a brain-damaged vegetable. I would feel very ashamed after taking an overdose. It would hurt my parents, my sisters, and a number of friends who have all been very kind to me recently.

(h) To move house and go ex-directory, so that nobody can find me. Pros: It would definitely decrease hassle. Cons: I don't want to move house, and I need friends and support.

(i) To explain to my mother that, although I do appreciate her opinion on a lot of issues, I think on this occasion she is wrong in trying to make up my mind for me. To explain to Phil that I do not want to be his girlfriend, but I do want to remain his friend. Pros: I would continue to get support from both my mother and Phil. I would get the space to get over Ian. Cons: It might be quite difficult to talk to my mother and Phil, and there is the danger I will hurt them. I will still be left with a lot of sad feelings for Ian and won't have an instant relief from them.

Step 4: In considering her options more closely, Andrea realised that she didn't want to become Phil's girlfriend again, and she firmly rejected Option (a). She also rejected options (b), (c), (e), (f), (g), (h), which, she felt, all had an element of running away in them. This left her with two options: (d) and (i). She felt there was still a strong pull towards being back with her old boyfriend, Ian, and she therefore looked at this option in detail.

Option (d) was to beg Ian to make a new start. Pros: If he took me back, I'd be unbelievably happy. But would I really? I still would be left with all the hurt over how he told me he didn't want to see me any more and with the worry that he might decide to dump me again like a hot potato, as he did before. Cons: If he said no to me I would feel even more hurt than now. Could I actually stand it to be rejected by him again?

Andrea remained unsure whether or not to take up this option. She decided to shelve it for two weeks, and if, after that, she still wanted to contact Ian, she might.

She then considered Option (i). She thought: "There is nothing to stop me from getting on with that now. Whatever happens with Ian, I need to sort things out with my mother and Phil."

Steps 5 and 6: She decided to tackle Phil first, which, she knew, would be easier. She told him that she appreciated his friendship and would always do so, but that she felt he was looking for more than that from her. She told him she did not want to become his girlfriend again, especially as she still felt very cut up about Ian.

She knew she was going to find it difficult to talk to her mother, and, in preparation, she jotted down on a piece of paper what she wanted to say: "Mum, I need to talk to you about something that is bothering me. You know I am still pretty upset about Ian, and you have been a great help with listening to me so patiently. But there is one thing that is not helping. You keep inviting Phil round to cheer me up, but it just doesn't work. It would help me more if you stopped doing that." She considered how her mother might react to this. There was some risk that her mother would get very upset and cross. Andrea thought it would be crucial that she chose a good time for them to discuss the issue and that, even if her mother did get upset, she would not hold it against her for the rest of her life.

She waited until she and her mother were alone at home on a Saturday afternoon and both quite relaxed, and then she approached her. As she had predicted, her mother was very upset. She said that she had only wanted to help, that Andrea was accusing her of matchmaking, which she had never tried to do, and that in future she would leave Andrea to sort out her own problems. Andrea left her mother feeling quite shaken up but still convinced that she had done the right thing.

Step 7: Her mother did stop inviting Phil around and making references to him, and two weeks later she even apologised to Andrea for having tried to interfere in her life. Phil continued to ring Andrea frequently, but somehow their conversation had cleared the air, and she no longer felt so pressurised by his phone calls.

Andrea's example shows that often there is no neat solution to a problem and that, like Andrea, in choosing an option, you may choose some risks and problems too.

FURTHER READING

Honey, P. (1983). *Solving your personal problems.* London: Sheldon Press.

CHAPTER THREE

Dieting: A Health Warning

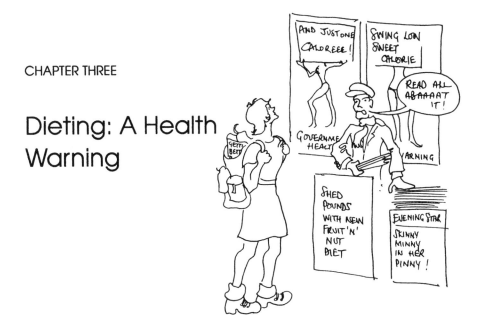

BEAUTY IS IN THE EYE OF THE BEHOLDER

What is considered to be the ideal female form has varied over time. Fashion thrives on change. What will be the preferred female body shape in five years' time? At any point in time, only a tiny minority of women will fit in with what is considered to be a fashionable shape.

Rosamund

Rosamund, a 17-year-old budding ballerina, was told by her principal that her technique and presentation were excellent, but that she had a problem—her breasts were too large. She was advised to consider plastic surgery to reduce their size. She was very upset by this report. She wanted eventually to marry and have children. Would this mutilation for the sake of her art interfere with this? Dieting seemed the only answer. She restricted her intake severely, but bulimia quickly developed, and her weight increased rather than fell.

These powerful messages and drastic remedies do not just affect women.

Stephen

Stephen, a builder, lost a foot in a car accident. He became interested in health and fitness and went to the gym to train regularly. Friends there suggested that he use steroids to build up his muscles. He did, but his family and girlfriend became concerned about the change in his personality. He became more irritable and lost his temper at the slightest provocation. One day, whilst driving, he became enraged when overtaken by another car. He set off in pursuit, despite his girlfriend's protests. She died in the resulting car crash.

Several examples of murders committed by men taking anabolic steroids have been reported.

The dangers, sacrifices, and mutilations to which people submit themselves for the sake of some ideal of beauty are astounding, especially when the goals are not shared with others. But perhaps this is part of human nature.

With the loss of beliefs in gods and fate, the whims and chances of nature are more and more considered to be under personal control. No longer do we say "she has all the luck", "the gods smiled on her". Any deviation from normality is blamed upon mistakes, neglect, and bad practices. You, too, can be beautiful if you only try hard enough or spend enough money and time on potions, practices, and surgery.

WHAT WEIGHT IS HEALTHY?

Table 3.1 gives the weight ranges (for different heights) into which the majority of people fall. As with height and shoe size, there is a large range of weights that are healthy. Some people are heavier than others, just as some people have bigger feet. (The current fashion of slimness is

TABLE 3.1
The Weight Band that is Appropriate for Your Height

Height (ft/ins)	Height (metres)	Weight (stone)	Weight (kg)
5' 0"	1.50	7st 2 to 8st 12	45–56
5' 1"	1.52	7st 4 to 9st 2	46–58
5' 2"	1.56	7st 8 to 9st 7	48–60
5' 3"	1.58	7st 11 to 9st 9	49–61
5' 4"	1.61	8st 1 to 10st 1	51–64
5' 5"	1.63	8st 3 to 10st 3	52–65
5' 6"	1.66	8st 7 to 10st 10	54–68
5' 7"	1.68	8st 12 to 10st 13	56–69
5' 8"	1.70	9st 2 to 11st 5	58–72
5' 9"	1.73	9st 7 to 11st 11	60–75
5'10"	1.75	9st 9 to 12st 2	61–77
5'11"	1.77	10st to 12st 7	63–79
6' 0"	1.80	10st 1 to 12st 9	65–81

perhaps no stranger than the ancient fashion in China for women to have small feet. The crippling bandages are now replaced by diet strait-jackets). Extreme overweight and underweight is associated with ill health and a short life.

If your weight is above the weight band given for your height, you should have a look at chapter 7 which has been written specially for you.

What Weight is Right for Me?

The weight and shape you are is determined mainly by your physical constitution. The genes you inherited, which programme your body, cannot be changed. To assess the weight and shape you may have inherited:

- Draw your family tree in your diary, and write in all the weights and heights of your family members.
- Collect photographs of your grandmothers, grandfathers, great-aunts, mother, father, aunts, and uncles when they were your age. Paste them in an album.

Enid

Enid came from a plump family; her mother, aunt, and grandmother had all been stout. She developed early and was bigger than all her school friends. She was ashamed when her periods began whilst she was at junior school. She started to diet when she read on the back of a packet of tights that her ideal weight was 2 stone below her current weight. She never reached that weight, because bulimia began.

If, like Enid, you come from a family in which most members are plump, it is likely that your healthy weight is at the top end of the normal range.

Muscles and bones are much denser than fat tissue. If you are an athlete, or the rest of your family have an athletic build, you should also expect your weight to be at the top end of the normal range. Similarly, if everyone in your family is big-boned, it is likely that you, too, should be at the top end of the normal range.

For many sufferers of bulimia, achieving a healthy weight simply means going back to the weight they were before their eating problems began. For some of you this message will be hard to swallow.

Are Weight Fluctuations Normal?

A person's weight normally goes up and down over time by about 4 to 5 lbs (2 kg) or more. If your weight goes up 5 lb one day, it does not follow that it will continue to do this.

Rapid weight changes are not normal but do occur as part of bulimia nervosa due to fluid shifts (chapter 5). It is therefore pointless to try to check and control your body by weighing yourself daily.

- Be bold: give your scales away, or put them in an place where you can't reach them easily (the loft or the cellar).
- Or, if you aren't quite brave enough to do that, draw up a timetable with plans for a gradual reduction in the number of times you weigh yourself.

Is Weight the Only Important Indicator of Health?

No. Recent research shows that the ratio of your waist measurement to your hip measurement is a better predictor of health than is weight. Your waist size divided by your hip size should be less than 0.9, i.e. your waist should be less than nine-tenths of your hip size. The traditional pear shape of women, although currently devalued, is a shape associated with health and a low risk of illness.

Cavemen Didn't Eat Ice-cream

Evolution and our genes have not yet caught up with two new things in our environment to which we now have to adapt: (1) Most of us have little or no exercise. (2) Our diet contains a high degree of fat, with high-fat items being promoted as special, luxurious, romantic, or even sexy (think of those ice-cream ads). In other words, it is much easier to get fat while leading a modern Western life style than if you were Neanderthal man.

Diets Don't Work

The greatest pressure to lose weight is on those members of our society who have a tendency to being overweight as part of their constitution. One conclusion drawn at a recent conference on obesity by the eminent scientist, Dr Kalucy, was that DIETS DO NOT WORK. He instructs all his obese patients to stop dieting, and they subsequently lose weight. Can this be true? All diets used to treat obesity can produce a 5% weight loss in the short term, but after a year the weight increases again to its normal, higher value.

- Go to your local bookshop, and see how many books and magazines there are on slimming and diets. How can there be such a big market for these items? Why are new diets and diet books published each year? The answer is, of course, that they do not work. Slimming is marketed as any other hobby, something that will entrap you for life.

Even doctors are affected by the propaganda, and they may suggest to you that a lower weight may be healthy for you.

Georgina
Georgina went to her general practitioner with a problem with her feet. He weighed her and said that she was overweight. She began to diet and lost weight, but soon she developed bulimia. Twenty years later she presented to a specialised clinic; her teeth were destroyed, and surgeons were advising her to have her large intestine removed to remedy her chronic constipation and stomach pain as a result of chronic abuse of laxatives.

THE HEALTH HAZARDS OF DIETING
Recent evidence from a large study in America, reported in *The New England Journal of Medicine*, shows that people whose weight has fluctuated often or greatly—i.e. who have gone on many diets—have a higher risk of dying from heart disease. The conclusion from this study was that the risk of early death was as high in those who went on many diets as in those who were massively obese. This was particularly important in the youngest group of patients.

Dieting is Dangerous
Weight loss has profound effects on your physical and psychological health.

The Effects of Starvation on the Body
1. Sensitivity to cold: this includes cold extremities, which may lead to chilblains.
2. Sleep disturbances: waking up early or several times in the night.
3. Weak bladder: passing water frequently throughout the day or night.
4. Excess hair growth on the body.
5. Poor circulation, slow pulse, and fainting spells.
6. Thin bones: with time this may result in fractures, leading to pain and deformity.

7. Periods stop or become very irregular. It is usually only possible for a woman to have periods when 15% of her body is composed of fat.
8. The stomach shrinks and feels uncomfortably distended after eating even a small amount of food.
9. Gut function is decreased, and constipation results.
10. The bone marrow, where the red and white cells in the blood are formed, is sluggish, which can result in anaemia.
11. The lack of nourishment to the liver damages it so that it is unable to manufacture body proteins. This may result in swelling of the ankles and legs.
12. The blood cholesterol level is increased. This results from the lack of oestrogen (women before their menopause are protected from heart attacks by oestrogen) and because of abnormal liver function.
13. General tiredness may lead to muscular weakness and paralysis.
14. In young girls, growth may be stunted and puberty delayed.

The Effects of Starvation upon the Mind
1. Mood is lowered, with tearfulness and pessimism.
2. The mind becomes preoccupied with food, and there is often a strong urge to overeat.
3. The ability and interest in forming relationships is diminished.
4. Concentration is poor, and it is difficult to function fully.
5. Minor problems appear insurmountable.
6. Complex thought is impaired.

These lists are very dry and dull, but many authors have written about the effects of starvation. We suggest you read *One Day in the Life of Ivan Denisovich* by Alexander Solzhenitsyn, Kurt Vonnegut's *Slaughterhouse-five*, and *Castaway* by R. Irwin, to see how starvation affects human thinking and behaviour.

You may say: I did lose weight when my problem started, but since then I have put on weight. So can the problems above still apply to me? The answer is yes, definitely, as a common pattern is to alternate fasting with bingeing. If you don't eat for over four hours, your body will start to go into starvation mode and switch all the metabolic processes to those that conserve energy.

HOW MUCH DO I NEED TO EAT?
Appetite is tightly linked to energy expenditure. This is known as metabolic rate. Your body has to work harder and will need more energy when you exercise or if you are in a cold climate. Hormonal changes in our body also affect metabolism. Women in the second half of their menstrual cycles are metabolically more active as their bodies prepare

themselves for egg implantation. One sign of this increased metabolism is the increase in body temperature seen after ovulation. You may have been aware of your increased appetite premenstrually and are frightened by it.

You can see from the above that there are no easy rules. People differ in the amount of energy they need, and all the factors mentioned above alter your energy requirements. As soon as you cut down your food intake, your body will clamp down on its energy expenditure, and losing weight will be more difficult. Your body will do this more quickly and more efficiently the more times you try to diet. This has been called weight cycling and has led a wit to describe it as the "rhythm method of girth control".

You should need to eat at least between 1,500 and 2,000 calories per day. However, if your levels of activity are high or you are still growing, you may need considerably more. However, we suggest that you do not try to count calories but judge portion sizes from those that other people eat or those available to be bought.

WORKING WITH YOUR BODY TO OBTAIN YOUR OPTIMAL WEIGHT AND SHAPE

Long gaps between meals switch the body into storage mode, and so nutrients will be selectively deposited in storage depots on the expectation of famine. The balance between fat and lean body tissue is disturbed, and so weight may increase to keep the amount of lean tissue constant. Eating only at night does the same sort of thing. At this time the body's hormones prepare for the fast during sleep and promote storage of energy into fat deposits.

Imelda

Imelda came to London from Northern Ireland to marry her boyfriend. She quickly had a baby and found it difficult to keep contact with her old work colleagues. Her husband's friends were not very welcoming towards her, and she felt very isolated. With her family in Northern Ireland, she had nobody she could turn to for help. Her eating became chaotic. Each morning she would wake up and vow to eat nothing, and, indeed, she would eat no meals. However, when she came home after finishing her shopping, having eaten nothing all day, the prospect of her son turning the sitting room to chaos led her to eat 6 to 7 bags of crisps, followed by a chocolate bar. To make up for this, she would redouble her efforts to avoid meals the next day. All the time her weight increased steadily.

To work with your body, you need to:

- Eat the majority of your food before evening.
- Eat small amounts regularly throughout the day.
- Exercise regularly, though not excessively.
- Restrict your consumption of fat but ensure that protein and carbohydrate are adequate.
- Avoid multiple courses.

Making a Start

The first step to get your eating under control is to ensure that you are eating regularly throughout the day. You may say, "If I start eating in the morning, I will binge all day." Yes, you are right, there may be a brief phase when you will be unable to stop eating after a meal, and you will have to take extra precautions, but the goal of regular meals throughout the day is essential.

You must not try to lose weight at this stage. If you do, the vicious circles of bulimia will just go on and on. You may say, "I can't give up trying to lose weight. It is too important." Yes, it is very tough to let go of something that is very important to you. Perhaps it is easiest if you just persuade yourself to put losing weight on hold for a while (a day, a week, a month, 6 months at a time). That way, it will be less frightening.

Also, once your eating is less chaotic, your weight may decrease, or the balance between fat and lean tissue may get more acceptable.

Plan A: For Those without Any Pattern to Their Eating

- If your eating pattern is totally chaotic, set a goal of re-introducing regular meals one by one. For example, could you manage a baked potato with cottage cheese for lunch? Do not be too ambitious, but do be honest with yourself. Choose something you feel safe in eating, preferably with safeguards to end the meal. Can you promise to eat this item every day? Expect it to be two steps forward and one back. Keep persisting. Every normal meal you eat is a small victory.
- Draw up a list of ten small meals that you think would be easiest for you to attempt to eat.
- Rank them in order of difficulty, with the most difficult at the bottom.
- Start with the meal at the top of the list.
- Plan to eat that meal at some time in the day before 3 p.m.

How can you ensure that this will not lead to a binge?
Ask yourself:

- Could I eat the meal with someone else?
- Could I eat this meal in a canteen or cafe?

- Could I have something I enjoy doing timetabled for half an hour after my meal?

YOUR ANXIETY AND GUILT LEVELS BEFORE, DURING AND AFTER THIS MEAL WILL BE HIGH. To deal with anxiety and guilt:

- Take a piece of paper or booklet and a pencil.
- Draw a vertical line and mark it 0–10 (0 = no anxiety; 10 = utter panic or overwhelming guilt)
- Put a mark where your anxiety/guilt level is now.
- Every 5 minutes, mark off what your level of anxiety/guilt is whilst eating and for 2 hours after eating.
- What exactly are the thoughts going through your mind now that are leading to these emotions? These thoughts may be vague and jumbled—that doesn't matter. Jot them down, even if they seem incomplete, frightening, or silly.
- Try to keep adding to the list over the next few hours.
- The next day, when you repeat your meal, take out your book and repeat this process—and so on, every day.
- Later, when you are relaxed, take out your booklet and paper, and re-read these thoughts that you have written.
- Either show them to a close friend, or imagine showing them to a close friend.
- What would they say about your thoughts about food?
- Get them to read this chapter. What would they say now about your thoughts?
- Write down exactly what they would say in your book.
- At the end of their replies to each of your list of thoughts about eating, indicate on a scale of 0 to 10 how much you agree with what they have said.
- Repeat this process each day.
- Try to catch any new thoughts you may have when faced with food.
- Try to make up your own replies to these ideas.
- Keep eating exactly the same meal each day with the same routine until your anxiety level at the beginning of the meal has fallen by at least 2 points. Then you may be ready to try to eat the next item on your list.
- With the next meal, go through exactly the same procedure as before. Once you have been able to tackle two different meals, try to eat two meals before 3 p.m. each day. Go through exactly the same procedure as before. The next stage, thereafter, will be to have two meals and a snack before 3 p.m. each day. Do not worry if your diet is rather monotonous at the moment.

Plan B: For Those with Some Degree of Order to Their Eating
If your eating pattern is reasonably regular, what is the size of your
meal? Are you eating sufficient calories early in the day?

- Gradually plan to shift your eating so that more calories are eaten
  earlier in the day. You should aim to eat 30% at breakfast and 40% for
  lunch.

HOW TO RELEARN EATING CONTROL

- Try to eat in a room that is separate from where food is stored and
  prepared. Eat all your meals in this place.
- Make every meal look as appetizing and attractive as possible.
- Lay out a table-cloth or place-mat and serviette.
- Make your place setting as attractive as possible.
- Bring your plate in from a different room, leaving behind all the food
  containers in the other room.
- Don't distract yourself with television, radio, or reading. This 15
  minutes is set aside to relearn about food.
- Spend 30 seconds looking at your plate before you begin. Put down
  your knife and fork between each mouthful. What does the plate look
  like now? Make sure you know how the food tastes and feels in your
  mouth. Take longer before you swallow.

What Should I Eat and When?

The ideal target is three meals almost equally divided calorifically and
each well balanced for protein (e.g. cheese, eggs, meat, fish, beans) and
carbohydrate (e.g. bread, pasta, potatoes, rice), with small snacks in-
between.

Remember these tips:

- Protein is more satisfying, calorie-for-calorie, than other food items.
- Hot food is more satisfying than cold food.
- Solid food is more satisfying than liquid food.

Ensure that there is no gap longer than 3 hours without a small snack,
e.g. coffee and some fruit.

Table 3.1 shows the diet plan of Thelma, who had gained weight with
bulimia. She was pleasantly surprised that she lost weight following
this plan.

TABLE 3.1
Thelma's Diet Plan

Time	Meal	What eaten
8.15	Breakfast	Fruit juice, 1 individual box of cereal, 200 ml skimmed milk, 1 slice of brown bread, 1 pat margarine, 1 spoon marmalade, 1 pot of tea or coffee
10.30	Mid-morning snack	Coffee with milk (skimmed), 1 piece of fruit
12.30	Lunch	Main course: piece of grilled meat with rice and salad or vegetarian dish Pudding: yoghurt, fruit salad or fruit, 1 cup of tea/coffee
3.30	Mid-afternoon snack	Tea with skimmed milk, piece of fruit or yoghurt or 2 plain savoury biscuits
6.30	Supper	Main course: same as lunch—fruit/yoghurt, 1 cup of water, 1 cup of tea with skimmed milk
	Bedtime	Hot drink with skimmed milk

- It may be easier if you follow exactly the same diet each day and gradually make exchanges so that the variety of your food is gradually increased, e.g. fish rather than chicken, or a pear for a snack rather than an apple.
- Take it slowly. It is difficult to change long-standing habits.

How Can I Judge What Amount to Eat?

You are right to think that this is difficult.

- Eat with other people, and have portions the same size as theirs.
- Buy individual meals (frozen or long-life).
- Avoid artificial sweeteners. These feed misinformation into your body. Your body is tricked by the artificial sweetener, and years of learning about the metabolic consequences of food is undone. Your body will learn: sweetness = no or little energy. Your body's instincts will therefore drive you to eat large quantities of sweet things as it strives for adequate nourishment.

How to End your Meals

There are many signals that the body uses to finish eating. All of these get upset with bulimia nervosa.

1. How a meal looks: all living creatures learn to predict how much energy and nutrients they will later absorb from a given food just by the look of it.

2. The taste and smell of foods are clues that remind our body what effect a given food will have on our blood sugar.
3. The feeling of fullness in our stomach is another sign to indicate that we have had sufficient nutrition.
4. Finally, hunger is satisfied for several hours by the nutrients that are absorbed into the blood.

As these normal ways of ending meals have been disturbed with bulimia nervosa, you may initially need to make triggers to end a meal.

Susan

Susan knew that whenever, and whatever, she ate, she would end up bingeing. She also could eat nothing with others, though she was able to confide in others and ask them to help. She asked her friend to knock on her door 15 minutes after starting a meal, go with her to put her food away, take her locker key, and sit and have coffee with her for an hour.

Alternatively, you could use food substances to signal the end of a meal.

Katie

Katie lived alone in a flat, and she devised a plan of eating a plain grapefruit at the end of each meal. The ritual of peeling, and then the sharp, bitter taste, was a powerful ending signal.

There are many other ways that you will be able to think of and use successfully. Spend some time thinking of alternative triggers, which you could use to end your meals.

CHAPTER FOUR

Bingeing, Nibbling, and Compulsive Overeating: The Black Hole of the Never-satisfied Stomach

The term "bulimia" means "eating like an ox". Most people with a bulimic disorder see binges as the central and most unpleasant aspect of their eating difficulties.

Andrew

Andrew, a 22-year-old student, described his binges as follows: "Once I've started, I stuff myself till I am completely full and bloated. I worry sometimes that my stomach might burst. I can hardly breathe. I eat very quickly, and I barely notice what I put into my mouth. I don't chew the food. The worst thing about it is this feeling of being totally out of control, of having to go on eating, it takes me over. I cannot stop until I'm absolutely stuffed."

People vary greatly in the kinds of food they eat during a binge and in the amount consumed. We define a binge as any large amount of food that is eaten rapidly in an out-of-control fashion. Mild bouts of overeating are part of many people's lives and are not unhealthy.

Other people don't exactly binge, but instead they follow a somewhat different pattern of overeating—so-called grazing or compulsive overeating, i.e. someone who nibbles all day without being able to stop.

Sonya

Sonya had a very difficult childhood, with her parents getting divorced when she was six. Thereafter her mother had a seemingly endless stream of boyfriends. "When a new man was on the scene, my mother hardly noticed my existence. They'd be out together most nights of the week. She'd give me lots of pocket-money though, to keep me quiet. After a while, things would go wrong, and there would be arguments, sometimes physical fights. Then the boyfriend would get kicked out, and I would be left with a mother who was miserable and bad-tempered, who withdrew to her bedroom for days. I had nothing to turn to apart from food. I remember sitting there day in, day out, eating one biscuit or sweet after another, to make that horrible loneliness go away. By the age of 13 I weighed 12 stone, although I am only 5 ft tall. At school nobody wanted to be my friend. So I ate more."

Even though Sonya now is in a stable relationship with a supportive partner, when he isn't around, she overeats. "My partner often has to go on business trips, he may be away for a few days at a time. When I am alone in the house I just eat all day, slowly and steadily. It is as if I constantly have to keep my hands and mouth busy. Sometimes I think it is to do with getting flashbacks of this old feeling of having nobody who cares. At other times I haven't got a clue why I do it, I just nibble all day".

In what follows below, we focus our discussion mainly on bingeing; however, if you graze, nibble, comfort-eat, or compulsively overeat, the descriptions below of the mechanisms involved will also apply to you.

Most people binge/graze/comfort-eat on high-calorie foods, which may be sweet or savory. Some people overeat on food that they secretly love but see as "unhealthy" or "forbidden" and therefore only eat during a binge. Others eat whatever comes their way, even food they don't like. Some people go as far as eating frozen food or scavenging through rubbish bins to find something to eat. The experience of overeating regularly is highly demoralising and makes most people feel that they have failed abysmally.

WHY IS MY EATING UNCONTROLLED?

Bingeing is not the result of being a weak-willed person. There are a number of important physiological and psychological reasons for bingeing.

Physiological Reasons

Bingeing can be the direct result of starvation. By giving you strong cravings for food, your body will tell you loud and clear that it is not getting enough nutrition. These cravings can be constant or intermittent. The harder you try to cut your food intake down, the more you will be prone to bingeing. Often people make things worse by cutting out meals after a binge to make up for having eaten so much. This will automatically programme the next binge. Alcohol and drugs, which reduce inhibitions, may also make you binge more.

Psychological Reasons

Boredom, depression, stress, tension, and loneliness often lead to bingeing, as food, at least at the start of a binge, is comforting and eases these negative feelings. Sometimes a small slip from a rigid and inadequate diet may make you so demoralised that you decide to give up control completely and have a binge.

Physiological and psychological reasons for bingeing are not mutually exclusive and often occur in the same person at the same time.

HOW TO STOP BINGES

A lot of people feel that if only their binges could be cured, they wouldn't have a problem. Unfortunately bingeing as a symptom can't be treated in isolation. In trying to tackle the physiological aspects of bingeing, it is very important:

- that you work on eating regularly at meal-times (see chapter 2) to give your body proper nutrition and thereby to reduce strong cravings for food that are going to set you off again;
- to try as hard as you can not to omit meals after bingeing, as this will programme the next binge.
- that you deal with the consequences of bingeing, e.g. vomiting (see chapter 5).

If you treat these aspects of your problem, you will soon find that binges decrease in duration and frequency.

Am I Addicted to Sugar?

Many people without an eating disorder have a sweet tooth. However, for sufferers of bulimia, cravings for sweet things can be so powerful that it feels like an addiction to sugar. You may also have the experience that, once you have had some sweets, you need to have more and more and more, reinforcing your sense of total powerlessness *vis-à-vis* sweets. Sugary foods are taken into our bloodstream more quickly than other foods. This increase in blood sugar leads to the hormone, insulin, being released, which facilitates the uptake of sugar into body cells, with the result that the blood sugar is lowered. Low blood sugar leads to the desire to eat more sweet things. This effect is particularly marked if you are undernourished. Also, if you drink large amounts of artificially sweetened diet drinks, your body will have learnt to associate the pleasant taste of sweetness with little nutritional value and will drive you to eat large amounts.

Some sweet foods, like chocolaty things, lead to the release of endorphines, morphine-like "happy-making" substances produced by the brain, making it very rewarding to eat this type of sweet.

However, you will find that if you follow the advice given in chapter 3 and work on eating more normally, the feeling of being addicted to sweets will lessen and even disappear completely, so there is no need to give up sweets altogether. As long as your eating pattern is very chaotic, it is probably wise to be careful with sweets and only to eat them in conjunction with some other food (to avoid getting low blood sugar after eating the sweet). Once you have a bit more control over your eating, to have a small amount of chocolate or cake every day may be a task to set yourself, to prove to yourself that you can tackle danger foods.

Dealing with the Psychological Aspects of Bingeing

You need to get to know your own triggers, which will be influenced by your body and mind. Your diary will help with this (see chapter 1). Here are some examples from former sufferers:

Anna

Anna, a 23-year-old woman, had a long journey to work, during which she had to change buses several times. "Each time I got off the bus, I walked past one or two sweet shops and I'd buy myself something else." Because Anna knew that she would binge on her journey to work, she never allowed herself any breakfast.

Anna decided to have a regular breakfast before going out. She also realised that she got extremely bored on her long bus journey (she couldn't read on the bus as this made her feel sick). Her solution to this was to find an alternative route, which meant she could take the train and read. These simple measures improved her bingeing greatly.

Belinda

Belinda started work at lunch-time. Mornings were a boring, unstructured time for her. There was nobody to have breakfast with as she liked to get up late and her mother was up very early. Sometimes Belinda would exercise in the morning, which she didn't enjoy but felt was good for her. However, when she was tired after a late night, she could not motivate herself to do her exercise, and she would have a binge instead. Belinda's solution was to do something she liked before work that would get her out of the house. She arranged to attend acting lessons in the morning, and her bingeing improved.

Ros

When Ros came to our clinic, she binged four to six times a week. Binges could happen at any time during the day, in different places. There did not seem to be any particular pattern. She felt very out of control and couldn't say what triggered her binges. She was asked to put into her diary a minute account of everything that happened from the moment she first had the thought of bingeing to the moment when she actually binged. It became clear that very often before an actual binge there would be a build-up of several hours during which small things would go wrong. This would lead to increasing frustration and would often result in a binge. On one day, for example, she was bored at work. At 2.00 p.m. she thought of bingeing for the first time. She rejected the thought firmly and distracted herself with a computer game. By 4.00 p.m. she was bored again, and the thought of bingeing came back. A friend then rang and cancelled their evening outing. At that point she went to the bank and drew some money out to buy food for her binge. She then made an attempt to contact another friend to go out but was turned down. By that point she was so upset that she went home and binged.

Over a period of time Ros became very good at identifying "danger" situations. She realised that she had used bingeing as an easy solution to many minor irritations in her life. For each "danger" situation she learnt to find a more appropriate way of dealing with it. For example, boredom at work was a recurring problem (she was a receptionist, and there were long stretches of sitting about without doing anything). She decided to do some reading towards a part-time degree course whilst at work, so that she didn't feel she had wasted the whole day. She decided that if friends let her down for evening arrangements, she would go to the cinema on her own instead, rather than sit at home and mope which would invariably lead to a binge.

The example of Karen, shows that even if you understand the psychological reasons for your binges, it may not always be easy to give them up very quickly, especially if there is a strong element of comfort.

Karen

Karen was a single working mother in her thirties. She had been sexually abused as a child. When she first came to see us, she binged and vomited several times a day. She then learnt to eat more during the day and only binged and vomited once at night, which she was very pleased about. She kept saying she wanted to improve more and give up bingeing and vomiting altogether, but somehow she couldn't. After a lot of discussion about why she had got so stuck at this point, it turned out that she felt her life was a constant struggle. She greatly missed having a partner who cared for her, but at the same time she was extremely frightened of entering a relationship with a man, given her traumatic childhood experience. She identified that bingeing was the only thing in her life that was easy, pleasurable, and comforting and made her lonely evenings more bearable.

These examples show that there are many different patterns of bingeing. You may need to monitor yourself using your diary for one to two weeks to get to know your own pattern.

- Once you have got to know your pattern a bit better, try to "play around" with it a little to increase your sense of control. Try to limit your binges to just one place. Alternatively try to restrict your bingeing to just part of the day.
- Write down a list of situations that trigger your binges and find ways of dealing with them.
- Try to anticipate danger-zones. Weekends with a lot of unstructured time are prime bingeing time for many. Draw up a time-table of pleasurable activities for the week end, and stick to it.
- Whenever you feel like bingeing, distract yourself by doing something that is incompatible with bingeing, like going for a walk, phoning or seeing a friend. Watching television and reading are not very helpful in this respect, as it is very easy to binge whilst you are watching. Many of the adverts are designed to promote dissatisfaction with ourselves as we are or encourage us to consume more.
- Don't do your food shopping when you are hungry.
- Don't get your parents/partner/flat-mate to lock the kitchen door. This is bound to make you want the food inside even more, and you will almost certainly find a way in.
- Don't blame yourself if you have had a binge. Look carefully at the behaviour chain, and spot the links that you could have broken. Work through in your mind what would have happened if you had made a shift. You will have learned something for next time (go to chapter 8, which discusses slips).
- A lot of people get very frightened if they haven't binged for a while. They feel that any binge would send them back to "square one". To prove to yourself that this is not the case, it is often useful to have a

planned binge. Remember, a small setback can't undo the good work you have done for weeks.

- Try to avoid people, places, and things that are associated with bingeing for you.
- Get in touch with someone you know who has had bulimia and has been able to control it. Find out what worked for them.

Coping with Cravings and Urges

- Monitor your urges to eat, and rate their severity (on a 1–10 scale) and duration.
- Make a note of what effect your expected eating would have on your thoughts, feelings, and physical state, as discussed in the example of Cherry below.

Cherry

Cherry noticed that her urges to binge occurred when she was lonely. She had not gone out with the rest of the family but had stayed at home to study. She wrote in her diary that she expected that a binge would get rid of her loneliness and her anger about having to work.

When you review your diary by yourself or with your support, try to draw up a list of the activities that would produce the effect that you sought when you binged. Some of your urges to eat will be started by the normal drives of appetite in response to hunger. Others are started by external factors. Urges are an entirely normal reaction, and you will need to develop several different strategies to deal with them.

- *Detachment:* Do not identify with the urge. Instead of thinking "I'm dying to binge", change your thoughts to "I'm experiencing an urge to overeat—it will get strong but then it will go". Allow yourself to experience the urge, "let it be". You don't have to give in to it. You may believe that if you don't give in to the urge, you will go mad or some other catastrophe will occur—it won't. If you do not give in to the urge, it will eventually weaken and go away.
- *Imagery:* Imagine that the urge to eat is like a wave. Let yourself surf along the top of the urge without losing your balance. Don't let the force of it suck you under.

  Imagine the urge as an ALIEN MONSTER. As soon as you recognise its presence, dispose of it quickly by chopping off its head.

  Imagine the urge as a growth inside you. You are a surgeon with a scalpel who can cut it out.
- *Logic:* Whenever you start to think of the positive short term benefits of eating, counteract these thoughts by thinking about the long term negative consequences.

- *Distraction:* Make a list of alternative activities you can do to take your mind off the urge.

If your trigger is anger or frustration, other ways of coping may be more helpful. An assertive response may be needed (see chapter 11).

LAPSES

Lapses will occur—they are a definite and important part of recovery. Simply regard them as challenges or learning experiences. The most important thing is to take them in your stride and not think that you are back to square one.

What to Do if You Do Lapse

- Stop and think! Try to intervene as soon as possible, and extract yourself from the situation.
- Keep calm! Observe yourself with detachment. Your first reaction will be to feel guilty and blame yourself—let these feelings slowly ebb away. Remember, this is a normal part of recovery.
- Renew your commitment: Get out your balance sheet and letters, and study them again. Think of how far you have come. Remake your decision. You can be in control.
- Review the situation that led to the lapse. Were there early warning signals? Did you make an attempt to cope? What have your learnt for next time.
- Take charge: Put into play one of your coping techniques—and leave the house.
- Get help: Now is the time that your supporter can be of greatest value. Get in touch with your co-therapist immediately.

CHAPTER FIVE

Vomiting, Laxatives, and Diuretics : Have Your Cake and Eat It—Or Not?

You may have read, heard about, or even discovered for yourself other methods of controlling your weight apart from restricting intake. The commonest methods chosen are making yourself vomit or taking laxatives or diuretics. Often these methods of "weight-control" are started when a person feels that dieting alone doesn't have the desired effect, or once binges have begun. Part of you may feel, "I can have my cake and eat it"— however, this is far from the truth. Part of you is probably somewhat ashamed and worried about using these practices. You are right to be worried.

FACING THE FACTS

Let's go through the facts first. How good are these methods at controlling weight? Although vomiting may get rid of 30 to 50% of calories eaten, depending on how soon after eating you do it and on how long you have used vomiting as a regular practice, it never leads to sustained weight loss. The more you vomit, the more your body will crave food. This will result in more bingeing, which then makes you want to vomit more. A vicious circle has started ...

Laxatives and diuretics do not lead to any loss of calories. Yes, you are right, they may reduce weight, but this is only temporary, and it is due to loss of body fluid. Your body protects against loss of water by producing a variety of hormones called anti-diuretic hormone, aldosterone, and renin, which are released generously in response to any loss of fluid. These hormones then lead to water retention, which will make you feel bloated and heavy. You may even notice swelling around your eyes in the morning, in your belly, and, at the end of the day, in your ankles. This will make you want to step up the dose of the laxatives or diuretics you are taking. Another vicious circle ...

Taking laxatives regularly over a period of time makes your guts lazy and will give you constipation. Gradually you will have to increase the amount of laxatives you are taking. The more you take, the more constipated you will become. You have entered yet another vicious circle ...

WHY YOU ARE RIGHT TO WORRY

A number of health problems are commonly caused by these practices. You need to know about these:

- Vomiting, laxatives and diuretics lead to a loss of blood salts and water. This commonly produces CHRONIC TIREDNESS, WEAKNESS, INABILITY TO CONCENTRATE, DIZZINESS, HEADACHES and PALPITATIONS. You also need to know that EPILEPTIC FITS, IRREGULAR HEARTBEAT and KIDNEY DAMAGE may be caused by these practices.
- Stomach acid brought up by vomiting dissolves the enamel of your teeth. This makes teeth sensitive and vulnerable to cavities.
- Your salivary glands around your mouth may swell up because they are working overtime to produce more saliva when you vomit. Although this is not dangerous, it can be painful at times. It will make your face look fat and bloated. You may even look as if you have mumps. This may make you think you ought to lose more weight and may make you vomit more. Another vicious circle ...!
- Vomiting may damage your gullet. Stomach pain and vomiting blood are common. Regurgitation of food may become habitual.
- Chronic laxative use may destroy the small nerves in your gut, which may lead to gut paralysis. This is a potentially life-threatening complication, requiring surgical treatment. Your back passage may start to come down when you strain on the toilet.
- Circle which of these health problems apply to you:

Chronic tiredness	Vomiting blood
Hair loss	Dental problems
Weakness	Fits
Inability to concentrate	Irregular heartbeat
Dizziness	Constipation
Headaches	Bleeding from your bottom
Palpitations	Something coming down, down below
Stomach pain	Kidney stones

Bloating	Kidney infection
Kidney failure	Ankle swelling
Irregular periods	

Most of these problems are reversible and will improve quickly if vomiting and the use of laxatives and diuretics are stopped. If none of these medical problems apply to you at the moment, you may feel somewhat reassured. You should bear in mind that some of them take time to develop.

WHAT TYPE OF WEIGHT CONTROLLER ARE YOU?

People vary enormously in their attitudes to vomiting, laxatives, and diuretics.

Type A: Some people see it as a kind of physical necessity to make themselves sick. They do not see themselves as responsible or playing an active part in it. Take Carla, a 25-year-old actress, whose eating disorder had started when she was 15. "When I've binged I feel terribly full. I feel physically sick. It's agony. I don't actually make myself sick. I just bend over and the food comes out. It just happens."

Type B: Other people see vomiting/laxatives/diuretics as a kind of habit, a part of their daily routine.
Natasha: "Vomiting is just like brushing my teeth. I don't feel much when I do it. It makes me feel clean. I couldn't do without it."
Lily: "I always take five laxative tablets after every meal. I have got so used to it. I hardly think about it."

Type C: Yet other people find these practices very painful and humiliating.
Susan: "I hate sticking my head down the loo every day. I am so ashamed of myself. How did I get into this? How could I sink so low? Afterwards I feel totally devastated and tell myself it will never happen again. But then it does and all the agony starts again."
Sheila: "Yesterday I had a 5-hour binge. I panicked totally and took 80 laxative tablets. I spent the whole night on the loo. I was in such a lot of pain. I felt disgusted with myself and yet I couldn't help feeling I had somehow deserved it."

Circle which of these types describes your own response most accurately:

Type A   Type B   Type C   Other (describe):

If you feel type A or B describes what you feel about your vomiting, laxative or diuretic abuse, you should ask yourself whether it has always been like this. You have allowed yourself to become cut-off from the pain of it. You do need to try to get in touch with these feelings again. The more cut-off you are from the negative aspects (pain, danger, shame) of your vomiting or laxative/diuretic abuse, the more difficult it will be to stop.

HOW TO STOP VOMITING

Follow Plan A if you:

- only make yourself sick 2 to 3 times per week; or
- often induce vomiting several hours after bingeing; or
- sometimes don't vomit at all after bingeing.

Follow Plan B if you:

- vomit most days; or
- vomit after snacks, meals, and binges.

Plan A: You have quite a bit of control over your vomiting, even though it may not appear so to you. The following plan is designed to give you even more control.

- Look back over the last 2–3 weeks. What has been the maximum number of times you have been sick per week?
- Over the next week try to be sick once less often than the maximum number of times per week you were sick before.
- If you manage to do this easily, cut down the number of times of vomiting you "allow" yourself by one further episode the week after.
- If you can only do this with difficulty, repeat the same step until it becomes easier.
- Continue like this, cutting down every week or every other week, until you have stopped vomiting.

A bit of general advice before you start: always write your goal for the week into your diary at the beginning of the week and then try to stick to it. Try to stick to your goal exactly. But don't aim to change too quickly.

- If you have had an extra binge, try, if at all possible, to keep the food inside you. If that is too difficult, try at least to delay the vomiting. This will make you very anxious. Use the coping techniques described under Plan B.
- If you were sick more often than you had decided to be one week, go back to last week's goal. (Remember, getting better often involves taking two steps forward and one step back.) Maybe you were a bit too ambitious last week!

Plan B: You have become very used to making yourself sick as a way of dealing with anxieties about gaining weight and perhaps other anxieties too. To un-learn this will be difficult. At present you probably only know two modes of existing—either being painfully full or being completely empty. Most people without an eating disorder know many states in-between, which range from being slightly hungry to being pleasantly full after a meal. You need to get used to the "in-between states" again. This is best achieved by a step-wise delay of vomiting.

- Think back over the last week or two. On average, what is your time-gap between eating and being sick?
- Over the next week, try to delay being sick regularly for this length of time.
- The week after, increase the time gap a little, and so on. Move to a new, longer time-interval when you reliably achieve this week's goal.
- If you always vomit straight after eating, you may want to start with delaying vomiting for a very short time only, say 5 minutes each time. It is better to go for a modest target and achieve this reliably than to be too ambitious.

How to Cope with Your Anxiety

Delaying vomiting will make you very anxious. You will probably feel terribly bloated, and your fears about gaining weight will rise sky-high.

- The best technique for coping with anxiety is to try to distract yourself by, for example, ringing a friend, being with other people, going for a walk, or by using the techniques of detachment and imagery described in chapter 4. Going to the bottle bank and smashing a few bottles can be good fun and helps release tension. (Watching television or reading are usually less successful as there is always a loo nearby!)

Margaret
Margaret, a 35-year-old housewife and mother of two children, enjoyed needlework, and so she decided to use sewing as a distraction technique. Every time she felt like being sick, she knitted an extra square for a patchwork blanket. "Knitting helped me to keep my anxieties down. At the same time, to see the patchwork blanket grow made me feel that I had channelled my anxieties into something useful."

Judith
Judith, on the other hand, found a spiritual solution for herself. "Normally I would say the rosary when I wanted to be sick, but if the anxieties got very strong I went to my local church and prayed."

- It is important that you find something that might work for you!
- Some people find it useful to write down some reassuring or frightening statements on a card that they carry around with them. Some even compose a comic song or jingle in which they make a joke of themselves.

Elizabeth

Elizabeth was a very gifted singer. On hearing that vomiting might make her hoarse, she decided to write on a card, "I want to be a singer. I don't want to damage my voice. I don't have to rely on vomiting." Every time she wanted to be sick, she pulled out her card and read the statements out loud to herself. "To read the statements on the card aloud gave me more strength to resist."

Susan

Susan, who often took up to 100 laxative tablets in one go, wrote a card to herself, saying, "If I carry on like this I will damage my health severely. I must stop". She got this card out a few times when she felt the urge to take laxatives, but she soon gave up, as thinking about the health consequences of her laxative abuse just increased her sense of panic.

In writing a card, you can see from the example of Susan that it is often better to write down something that is specific to you (not a general statement) and also something positive, rather than focusing on the negative.

Golden Rules

- Try one thing at a time, for a week at a time.
- If you fail, make things easier and try again.
- Especially if you follow Plan B, it is very important that you find ways of rewarding yourself if you achieve your weekly target, as otherwise, with each weekly step being small, it may be difficult to remember that you are doing well. Here is a list of possible rewards from which you may want to choose. Think of ideas which you might add to the list. Buy yourself something nice:

      a book
      a bunch of flowers
      a plant
      some earrings
      a day in the country

- Until you have managed to give up vomiting completely, you need to know that YOU SHOULD NOT BRUSH YOUR TEETH IMMEDIATELY AFTER VOMITING, as it rubs in the acid and makes things worse. It is better simply to rinse your mouth either with water or with a bicarbonate or fluoride solution.

HOW TO STOP ABUSING LAXATIVES, DIURETICS, AND OTHER MEDICATIONS

Especially if you have been taking laxatives or diuretics on a daily basis in fairly large amounts, you may find that if you stop them suddenly, this will lead to "rebound" fluid retention, which can cause gross swelling. It may be easier to cut down your laxatives/diuretics gradually. You can do this either by cutting down on the number of laxatives you take each day or by gradually increasing the number of laxative/diuretic-free days per week.

Coping with Constipation

Giving up laxatives will invariably make you constipated for a while. This is bound to make you feel uncomfortable and bloated. Remember, many women are prone to constipation anyway and do not have a regular daily bowel movement.

- Including fruit and vegetables in your diet will help.
- A hot drink before eating in the morning stimulates the bowels.
- Do not eat too much bran, as this will result in stomach distention and flatulence.
- Replace laxatives on a one-to-one basis with prunes or other dried fruit.

Coping with Swelling (Oedema)

Despite cutting down your laxatives/diuretics gradually, you may still, for a while, be prone to developing oedema. To prevent this:

- Consider sleeping propped up, to avoid oedema collecting around the face.
- Try to sit with legs up to help the oedema drain from your ankles.

Learning to Feel Good about Your Body

Many people with bulimia feel extremely bad about their body. They treat it, not as a part of themselves, but as a hated enemy that they would like to get rid of. They constantly watch it, criticise it, and struggle against it. Many sufferers of bulimia can't face looking at themselves naked, touching their body, or having someone else get physically close to them or touch them.

Ruth

Ruth, a very pretty, petite 28-year-old woman, described her body as follows: "When I look at myself in the mirror, I see a grotesque monster. I see the wrinkles that are coming up in my face, my neck is like that of a turtle, my breasts are sagging, my stomach is huge, and my legs are flabby. My boyfriend says I have nothing to be ashamed of and quite a lot of other men pay me compliments about my appearance, but that doesn't make the slightest bit of difference to how I feel about myself. When I have a bath, I lock the door so that nobody can come in and see me. I undress and wash quickly; I can't stand being naked. It is too painful. I can't bear my boyfriend near me, let alone have him touch me. We haven't made love in months. I used to like pretty clothes, but now I just dress in big baggy jumpers to hide myself. I used to be a keen Morris dancer, but lately I couldn't face going any more. I can't bear the thought of all that loose flab wobbling around."

Perhaps you don't react quite as strongly as this. A specific trigger may make a person feel bad about their body, like a slight weight gain, or a feeling of premenstrual bloatedness, or for someone to make a remark related to your appearance.

Felicity

"I went to work wearing a new pullover. A colleague—whom I really like, said what a nice pullover I had. I immediately thought he meant "nice pullover on the wrong woman" and that he must have noticed how flat-chested I am. For the next three days I couldn't get rid of that thought. I have since avoided talking to him."

Barbara

"I often have people shouting nasty things after me as I walk along the road. I do absolutely nothing to provoke it. Most recently I walked past a building site. As I could see some men working there I crossed the road. They whistled and tried to get my attention. I just looked straight ahead, as if I hadn't heard anything. Then one of them shouted, "She's got a fat bum". They all laughed. Whenever something like that happens, it just brings out all my insecurities about my physical appearance, I feel totally unattractive. If people you don't know bother to make comments like that about you, it must mean there is some truth in it, mustn't it?"

But even if you encounter stresses, tensions, or unpleasant events that are nothing to do with your appearance—say, your boss criticises your work or you have a burst pipe in your flat—you may still respond by feeling bad about your body. For many eating disorder sufferers the way they feel about their body is the most sensitive barometer of how they feel about themselves and their life in general at a given point in time.

LEARNING ABOUT BODY SHAPES

- Go to your local art/archaeological/anthropological museum or to a library. Look at pictures or statues of women. See how their shapes have changed over the centuries and how they differ across cultures. Get some postcards of ancient Greek or Roman statues or of African tribal women. Pin them up above your bed. What do they make you feel?
- Go into a cafe and watch passers-by. Find someone who isn't slim like a fashion model and who you still think looks good. What does it depend on whether you think someone looks good? Their style of dress? Their posture? Their facial expression? Anything else?

- Start with one inch of your body towards which you can be tender. Allow yourself to pamper this part, e.g. rub in some cream or massage it. Gradually increase the area that you can treat in this way.

GETTING TO KNOW YOUR BODY

- Look at yourself naked in a full-length mirror. Look closely from head to toe; don't forget your ears and the soles of your feet. Take a hand-mirror to look at your back. What do you see? Write down three things you like about your body and three things you don't like about your body. Don't let yourself get away with not finding anything nice to say about yourself.
- Write down three things a close friend (male/female) and a stranger (male/female) might like about your appearance and three things they might not like.
- Close your eyes and touch and stroke your body, starting with your face, moving downwards, making sure you get a good feel of all the different parts. What do you feel? Is your skin rough or smooth, warm or cold, do you feel your heart beating, your ribcage move when you breathe, and your tummy rumble? Is it pleasurable or unpleasant or even frightening to do this?
- Stand against a wall. Press shoulders and head back firmly against it. What do you feel?
- Walk around as if you were very proud of your body, with your head upright. Make sure not to overstretch head or neck, as this will lead to neck ache and tension. (Walk as if you were suspended from a string).
- Put on your favourite slow piece of music and dance gently and quietly; now switch to your favourite fast record or tape and dance as vigorously as you can, and then relax.

LOOKING AFTER YOUR BODY

If you don't like your body, you are likely to neglect it, to be out of tune with its rhythms, and to ignore its signals. Here are some suggestions as to how nurture it:

- Make sure you are getting enough sleep at night. Allow yourself some breaks during the day. Don't drive yourself on constantly.
- Draw up a list of things that you can do with or for your body/appearance and that make you feel good. How about walking, cutting wood, sunbathing, swimming, digging the garden, dancing, having a haircut, having a massage, soaking in aromatic oils? (If your list contains mainly vigorous sporting activities, think whether you are actually enjoying these things or whether they just make you feel good because they might make you lose weight.)

- Relaxation is another excellent way to recharge body and mind. The aim is to experience a state that lies between normal, day-to-day consciousness and sleep. If you liken your mind to a car, you want to achieve the state in which it is idling, in neutral, out of gear. There are several techniques for doing this, and some will suit you better than others, so try them all. Do not expect them to be easy or to produce magical solutions instantly. Like any skill (cycling, swimming, etc.), you need to practise regularly to master it.

Even with regular practice, some people find it quite difficult to achieve a state of relaxation. A relaxation tape can be a useful aid. You can make your own, by simply recording the instructions for the exercise below.

Relaxation Exercise 1 [1]
This exercise is based on Progressive Relaxation Training, a method of learning to induce a state of physical "relaxation" by tensing and relaxing groups of muscles in a systematic way. Find a comfortable chair to sit in. Loosen any tight clothing, take off glasses if you wear them, and ensure that you are warm enough. You are now ready to begin.

- Close your eyes and concentrate on your breathing. Take a deep breath in, hold it, and breathe out. Then repeat. Take a deep breath in, hold it, and breathe out. Keep your breathing rhythm steady. Do not breathe so fast that you get lightheaded. During the relaxation exercise you will be asked to tense and relax various muscles; you will find it easier to breathe in when tensing and breathe out when relaxing.
- Screw up your eyes as tightly as possible, clench your teeth, and purse your lips. Feel the muscles in your face tighten and then feel the tension fall away as you allow the muscles to relax. And again, as you breathe in, screw up your eyes tightly, clench your teeth, and purse your lips, and slowly breathe out as you allow your muscles to relax. Once more, tighten the muscles in your face and hold before slowly breathing out and letting the muscles relax.
- Keep breathing in a steady rhythm, and raise your shoulders to your ears. Allow your shoulders to fall as you breathe out. Repeat this twice more, feeling the tension in your neck and shoulders fall away.
- Now tighten your muscles in your upper arms like a strong person, and hold for a while before relaxing and breathing out. Tense the muscles in the upper arms, and feel how heavy they are when you relax them.
- Now clench your hands to make a fist, hold them for a while, and then relax. Again, make your hands into a fist, hold, and gently allow your fingers to uncurl.

- Take a deeper breath in, and feel the muscles in your chest and stomach being expanded. Hold and slowly breathe out. Repeat this deeper breath in, hold it, and breathe out. Allow your breathing to return to its gentle rhythmic pattern.
- Now tighten the muscles of your stomach, and gradually breathe out as you relax them. Again, pull in your stomach muscles, hold, and relax. Once more, tense your stomach muscles, hold, and relax as you breathe out.
- Now work the muscles on your lower back and buttocks. Tighten them, hold, and relax. And repeat this a further two times.
- As you take your next breath in, tighten the muscles in your upper legs. Keep the tension for a while, and then relax as you exhale. Tense this set of muscles twice more.
- Now point your toes up towards your body, and tense the muscles in your calves. Hold, and then allow your muscles to relax. Repeat this once more. Your legs and feet should now feel heavy.
- Continue to breathe evenly. Your body now feels relaxed and comfortable and is sinking into the chair with heaviness. Allow your mind to drift with pleasant thoughts.
- End the relaxation exercise by slowly opening your eyes and gradually moving your body, becoming aware of your surroundings. You will now be feeling calm, refreshed, relaxed, and awake.
- Practise this exercise two or three times a day. Once you feel you have mastered it, gradually reduce the groups of muscles you use until a state of relaxation can be induced by mental means with minimal muscle exercise.

Relaxation Exercise 2
- Close your eyes and start by taking a deep breath in, hold it, and gently breathe out. And again breathe in, hold, and slowly breathe out. Keep your breathing steady throughout this exercise.
- Imagine that your body is full of fine, soft sand and that you have small holes in your fingertips and toes. The sand gradually leaves your body through your toes and fingers. Feel the sand filter out of your body, and, as it does so, feel your body become limp and heavy.
- Allow your head to drop forward as the sand starts to leave your body. As the level drops, your arms and abdomen feel heavy and limp and sink into the back of the chair. You can feel the sand draining slowly from your legs and, as it does, the muscles in your legs feel relaxed and limp. As the final grains of sand fall from your toes, your whole body feels relaxed, comfortable, and heavy. Keep your eyes closed and your breathing slow and steady and allow your mind to drift away

with pleasant and peaceful thoughts. When you wish to end the relaxation exercise, gradually open your eyes and become aware of your surroundings. Gradually move your arms and legs. You will now be feeling calm, refreshed, relaxed, and awake.

LIVING WITH YOUR BODY

Living with/inside a body you don't like is difficult. Many of the people we see avoid getting on with their lives: they don't go out, they shelve having relationships, and ... and ... and ... . They all dream the same dream. "If only I ... —were slimmer, less pear-shaped, had thinner thighs, not such a big tummy, etc., my life would be completely different." Some people waste years like this.

Tragically, in the early phase of an eating disorder, some people achieve their ideal appearance for a short while through following a punishingly hard diet, and often this is remembered years later as the one good period in their life that they want to go back to at all cost. Only rarely do people allow themselves to remember how high the price they paid was.

June
"If I am honest with myself, it wasn't all rosy when I weighed seven stone. I thought about food day and night. I dreamt about it. I sometimes had nightmares about being force-fed. I felt guilty about absolutely anything I ate, I couldn't even eat an apple without regretting it. I remember having lots of arguments with my boyfriend. I think I was very irritable then. I lost my interest in music. Although a lot of people commented on how pretty I looked, my closest friends seemed to think I had undergone a complete personality change. I kept getting distracted, I couldn't concentrate, and I couldn't look at them when they talked to me. They didn't like it at all."

Women with eating disorders tend to overestimate the size of their body, the more out of control your eating is, the worse this gets. Working on your eating behaviour, therefore, will have a positive effect on your attitudes to your body. However, attitudes are much more difficult to change than behaviour, and they change much more slowly. So, even if you manage to get into a pattern of eating normally fairly quickly, your negative body image is likely to persist for a while longer. Be patient. You can't change everything overnight.

What you can do, however, is to work on those things you avoid due to feeling bad about your body. What is the point of wasting more time?

Susan

Susan made a list of all the things that she avoided. She wrote them down in hierarchical order, starting with the situations she feared most, progressing to the ones she feared least but still avoided. Here is her list:

- going swimming / to the beach in a bikini (impossible)
- dancing a slow dance with a man (very difficult to get physically close to someone)
- going to a party (difficult to meet new people and to know what to talk about)
- going to a restaurant with friends (worried what they will think about me if they see me eat)
- wearing tight skirts (worried about my stomach and lack of waist)
- wearing short sleeved T-shirts (because my arms are flabby)
- wearing brightly coloured clothes (fear this would draw attention to me)

- Make a similar list for yourself. Tackle an easy situation over the next week and a slightly more difficult one the week after. Include working on this in your weekly goals.

If you go ahead with this, don't expect to find it easy or to enjoy yourself at all initially. Expect to have a difficult, anxious, and very self-conscious time. It will take quite a bit of time before you can hope to feel more at ease with yourself. Getting better is about taking some risks. What do you have to lose?

NOTE

1. Adapted from Wanigaratne, S., Wallace, W., Pullin, J., Keaney, F., & Farmer, R. (1990). *Relapse Prevention for Addictive Behaviours*. London: Blackwell Scientific Publications.

FURTHER READING

Baker, N.C. (1984). *The Beauty Trap*. London: Piatkus.

Hutchinson, M.G. (1985). *Transforming Body Image*. Freedom, CA: Crossing Press.

Wolf, N. (1991). *The Beauty Myth*. London: Vintage.

CHAPTER SEVEN

Jack Spratt's Wife: Being Fatter May be Better

This chapter was written especially for those of you who, in addition to bulimia, have a problem with your weight, i.e. if your weight is above the top end of the weight band given for your height (in Table 3.1, chapter 3), you should definitely read this chapter.

Do you remember the nursery rhyme about Jack Spratt and his wife? "Jack Spratt could eat no fat, his wife could eat no lean … ." She is usually portrayed as fat, but happy.

In our society, it is hard to be rounded and happy. Long gone are the days of Rubens and large actresses like Marilyn Monroe and Jane Russell. If you are within the heavy half of the population, you will be put under constant pressure to go on a diet. Magazines, newspapers, acquaintances, and even your friends may make you feel morally inferior unless you try to do something to conform to society's idealised norms.

Josie
"I was a big child, and a big teenager. I weigh 18 stone now. I have had years of comments, abuse, and humiliation because of it. It is amazing anybody feels they have the right to tell me off because of it. The other day I went to a new GP because of an ear-ache. He briefly dealt with my ear and then gave me a long lecture on the health risks of being overweight, and then he sent me off to see a dietician." Josie also noticed: "As long as I try to lose weight, others

will be pleased with me, and I will get encouragement. If I ever eat a piece of cake in public, people comment: "Oh, I thought you were on a diet? Aren't you a bit naughty? Think of how nice you could look if you lost a bit of weight." Even if they don't say anything, I can see the disapproval in their faces. I can see they think, "she's letting herself go."

David Garner, one international authority, recently commented on the plight of the obese: "obesity is still one of the most stigmatized physical attributes in Western society today, leading to discrimination in a wide range of settings." He also commented that "It is time for greater emphasis on acceptance of fatness and concentration on the civil rights of the obese, with efforts at public education to counter the social stigmatization associated with fatness."

In 1992 in the United States, women's groups started to rebel against the diet dictators and began to smash weighing scales with the slogan, "Scales are for fish, not women".

THE HEALTH RISKS OF BEING OVERWEIGHT

A powerful message to people who are heavy is that they are damaging their health, and many diets are started upon medical recommendation. Public health campaigns have emphasised that obesity is linked to heart disease, high blood pressure, diabetes, joint problems, and even certain sorts of cancer. However, scientists now think that the seriousness of these risks has been exaggerated, certainly for people who are only mildly or moderately overweight. Being plump may actually protect you against some forms of disease. Newer research also has shown that it is not high weight, as such, but your weight yo-yoing up and down—as is common for many people who regularly diet—that may lead to heart disease and even death. People who are heavy and fit probably don't have more health risks than those who are thinner.

PIE IN THE SKY

You may say, "that's all very well, but I can't wait till society is more accepting of the kind of figure I have. I do want to lose weight." You will remember from chapter 3 that diets don't work. Any diet will increase the odds of you starting to binge eat. Your weight will begin to bounce up and down. This instability will lead to harmful metabolic patterns, with swings of insulin, fat, and sugar, and ultimately to your weight creeping up more and more. Thus a diet begun to improve health and beauty will have the opposite effect.

Samantha

    Samantha, a 23-year-old beautician, gained over 6 stone in weight during a three year-period, which had started as a stringent diet and then progressed into the yo-yo cycle of binge eating, with her weight gradually going up and up. See Figure 7.1

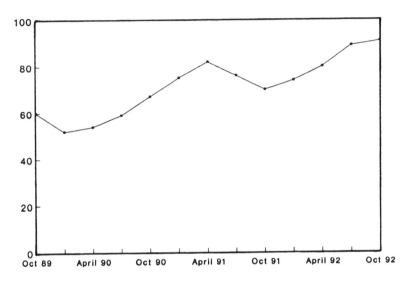

FIG. 7.1. Samantha's weight chart.

    So the painful truth is that you really have to stop dieting to get over binges and to allow your weight to settle to a level that is right for you. To face up to this is extremely difficult. Monitoring your eating pattern by means of a diary, as we have introduced earlier, is an essential first step. It is important to structure your daily intake into meals and snacks.

Alison

    Alison, a 24-year-old woman, found it impossible to control her eating. She would diet for one or two days and then spend the rest of the week bingeing. Her therapist told her that she must eat three meals a day plus three snacks, and that she could eat anything she wanted. "I was amazed. I realised that I had not been eating what I wanted for nearly all my adult life. I had been going from one diet to another, and here I was being told to eat regularly, and to eat anything I wanted, including potatoes, puddings, and sweets. I was totally surprised when after a week of doing this I had lost three kilos. I did not go on losing weight, but I managed to maintain my weight, which was the first time I had done that for almost as long as I could remember. After a couple of months, when I was really comfortable with eating regularly, my therapist suggested that it might be safe for me to cut down slightly. The way I did this was to make sure that I did not eat much more than 1700 calories a day. All that meant, really, was that I did not have huge great portions of anything, but I could continue eating all my favourite foods".

ONLY THE LONELY

Because of the stigma of being fat, secondary problems can arise with your daily life-style, career, social and family life and contribute to the downward spiral. You may have put your life completely on "hold", not wanting to have any form of pleasure or enjoyment while you are fat. Subjecting yourself to loneliness and misery because of what you think others will say is a sure recipe for disaster and will ensure that you keep slipping further over the edge. It is therefore important that you begin to set goals and structure your life to take this into account.

Samantha

Samantha, whom we introduced to you earlier in this chapter, was so upset by her weight gain that she stopped working as a beautician, as she felt very inferior to the other girls with whom she worked and she could not fit into her uniform. She restricted her social life more and more and only left home to go shopping by car. She felt miserable and alone. With encouragement from her therapist, Samantha decided that she would try to go out and socialise at least once a week, although the thought of this terrified her. The next week Samantha reported back to her therapist: "I did it. I went out to the pub. I was absolutely terrified, and when I got there I felt that everyone was looking at me, seeing how fat, ugly, and horrible I was. I went with my friend, and we sat at a corner table, but, do you know, after about ten minutes or so I had totally forgotten about everyone staring at me and I was able to relax and enjoy myself. I really had a lovely evening, and I am going to go out again next week."

SHAKE, SHAKE, SHAKE YOUR BODY

You may always have been someone who hated sport at school or who was laughed at, or ridiculed, for performing badly. You may be put off exercising because you feel you are not the right shape or size, and, like Samantha, you may want to hide away and isolate yourself from society.

Don't! You are not too fat to exercise. The variety of activities available to you is immense, and you can try different ones to find whatever is right for you. Regular exercise will probably not decrease your weight in a big way, but it can increase your metabolic rate and enable your weight to remain stable. Contrary to common belief, exercise does not increase appetite but slightly decreases it. Exercise also increases suppleness, strength, and stamina. It is an ideal method of dealing with stress. It can take your mind off your problems, and after a session of exercise you will feel warm, comfortable, and relaxed. It can thus replace overeating or purging, which, for many people with eating disorders, are their prime ways of coping with stress. Exercise can also lift depression and help sleep.

Remember:

1. Exercise can burn off calories.
2. It promotes health.
3. It can give you a sense of mastery, and so help you deal with stress.
4. It helps your weight to stabilise rather than go up.
5. It preserves body muscle.

Overcoming Obstacles

- The type of "all-or-nothing" approach to life that many people with eating disorders have means that they jump in at the deep end and do something to excess, which is painful and uncomfortable and then is not repeated. It is much better to start with something that you enjoy and build up the intensity slowly and gradually. It should not have to hurt to do you good. If it does you are pushing yourself too hard. If your breathing is uncomfortable, slow down.
- The need to please others and a fear of being selfish, which are other characteristics of people with eating disorders, may lead you to think that you have not got time to devote to something that is primarily for yourself. You do not need that much time. Just 20 minutes, two to three times per week, can be sufficient, and you may then find that, with practice, it becomes easy to put aside the time.
- Even if you have young children, you can probably find a way of getting more exercise. Many sport and leisure centres now have child-care facilities, and you can get details of these from your local Council Leisure and Recreation Department or your local library.
- Try to incorporate your children into your exercise schedule if possible, as this will set up good habits for them. You can take them in a pushchair when you go for long walks, or you can put them on your bicycle.
- Perhaps you could think of doing something that involves someone else. Could you persuade a friend to join you at a club or a class?

- Try to choose something that fits into your routine easily, so you can do it regularly. Don't take on something for which you have to travel far or that you can only do under certain weather conditions.
- The self-defeating "toad-in-the-hole" outlook on life (described in chapter 10) makes many people who are overweight avoid any form of exercise, as they fear that they will look ridiculous or that others will mock and jeer at them. Although there will always be an ignorant minority who think this way, people whose view you would respect would commend your enterprise and your bravery in facing a challenge and doing something positive rather than avoiding the problem.
- If you have a medical condition such as a heart problem or a muscle problem or simply are worried about whether exercise is right for you, go and discuss it with your general practitioner. There are, however, very few people for whom moderate exercise is dangerous.

How to Change Your Lifestyle to Get Fitter!

We need to repeat that an "all-or-nothing" or an "either I am perfect or I am useless" approach to life are totally out of place in the context of exercise. You do not have to start marathon running! An increase in mobility and stamina can be achieved by slight changes in your lifestyle through more walking and increased activity around your house and work.

The way to do it is to find more active ways of doing the things you usually do. Don't save things up to be efficient, do them as you think of them.

Walking

This is excellent and is available to all, with few risks of injury or strain. You can use your time whilst walking to observe, to think, to listen to music or a radio, to learn a language or to talk with a friend.

Apart from reasonably comfortable shoes, you do not need expensive equipment. To prepare yourself, put talcum powder on your feet (and tights), and afterwards persuade a friend to give you a foot massage or have a ten-minute soak in the bath with some aromatic oil in it.

Begin walking for 15 minutes each day, increasing by 5 minutes each day or week. If the 15-minute walk is too difficult, go for a shorter period initially. The goal should be to walk one hour each day.

By the way, walking burns off the same number of calories as running the same distance. How far you go is more important than how fast you go.

Think of ways of including walking in your life:

- Get up 30 minutes early to walk.
- Walk during lunch breaks.
- Walk after work.
- Walk before bed.

Experiment to find the best combination of place, time, and companionship for you.

Walking with a partner can be an excellent time for talking together without the distractions of television or newspaper. It can give you both time to unwind and to mull things over. You do not need to have a dog to have a regular walk around the block!

Try to include walking in your every-day pattern of life, but there is no need to despair if you miss the odd day. Try to plan your holidays with this in mind.

Using Stairs
Climbing stairs burns more calories per minute than do vigorous activities like jogging and cycling. It is very easy to incorporate the use of stairs into your lifestyle, because you can find stairs at home, at work, in shops, and on public transport, etc. In modern buildings it may take some detective work to find the stairs, but they will be there. One large American study by Dr Ralph Paffenbarger from Stanford University found that people who climbed only 50 stairs (not flights) each day had a reduced risk of heart attack.

Avoid using the lift whenever possible, or take it to the floor below where you have to go, so that you walk up the last flight. Use every opportunity to go up and down the stairs at home or at work. Try to ensure that you have to use stairs to go to the toilet or to make a drink.

Measuring Your Goals
The pulse test is a simple means of measuring your progress with exercise. Time your pulse every month. As you get fitter, your pulse rate in response to exercise should decrease. The pulse rate in untrained people is usually about 80 beats per minute.

How to do it: Wrap the fingers of one hand around the back of the other wrist. Press the index and middle finger on the upturned wrist until you can feel the pulsing of blood through the vessel. Count the number of beats in exactly 15 seconds.

Multiply the number by 4 to calculate your beats per minute. Take your pulse rate both at rest and during exercise.

If you want to get guidance on how to increase your activity, write to the Health Education Council to get a copy of their booklet "Exercise, Why Bother?" You can get it for free if you write to:

Publications Section
Health Education Authority
Hamilton House
Mabledon Place
London WC1H 9TX

Here is how some people with eating disorders have increased their exercise:

Samantha

Samantha was initially very pessimistic about trying to increase her exercise as she had tried to go to an aerobics class that she had attended before she had gained weight. Samantha was terribly upset to find that she could not keep up with even the easiest exercises in the class. Her therapist explained that she needed to start exercising very gradually, and, between them, they decided that ten minutes' brisk walking a day was all that Samantha should aim at. "When my therapist suggested ten minutes' walking a day, I thought that was absolutely hopeless. I felt that I ought to be exercising really, really hard for hours and hours or not bother to do anything at all. My therapist explained that my body would take time to readjust to exercise and that it was best to build up gradually. I was not really convinced, but I thought that I would go along with it as I had been so upset that I could not do the aerobics. What I started doing was go out for a walk in the evening with my friend when I felt that it had got a bit dark and people would not be likely to see me. We would walk for a little bit, and then I would say that it was time to do my ten minutes' brisk walking, so I would really increase the speed for ten minutes, and then we would slowly walk back to the house. I soon found that this was less of a challenge, and gradually I began to build up the amount of time I was spending walking briskly by five minutes each week. Just going out of the house made me feel less sensitive about people seeing me, and I started going out for walks during the daytime as well. It gave me such a good feeling to realise that I was doing something positive about my problem and not just sitting, waiting for it to go away."

Claire

Claire was a 29-year-old woman who found it very difficult to get any exercise as she worked as a telephonist and spent all of her day sitting down. "I just really did not know how I would get any exercise and fit it into my day. Then I had the idea of getting off the bus one stop early and walking that last little bit to work. I was amazed how exhausted it made me feel the first few days I tried it. It did get easier, though, and really my perseverance paid off, and I began getting off the bus two stops earlier, then three stops, and now a year and a half later I am cycling to work. I feel so virtuous when I cycle past the bus and see all these pasty faces in the window and think that used to be me."

Some Exercises to Do at Home

Lots of people prefer to exercise at home. It's private, and there's no need to get a babysitter or travel anywhere. However, you might get more out of it if you go to a class first and learn how to do the exercises properly. Below we describe six simple stretching exercises. Do them at least three times a week, and you'll begin to feel your body becoming more supple and relaxed. You should also do them to warm up before starting on anything more vigorous. Do all stretching exercises slowly and smoothly. Repeat each one 8 to 12 times. Doing them more times or more quickly won't have any extra benefit. You don't need to do 12 on the first day. Just do as many as you are comfortable doing, and gradually build up. If you have trouble with back pain, it might be advisable to see your doctor first. In any case, do these exercises very gently.

Arm Circling: This is to maintain suppleness in your shoulders.

- Stand tall and relaxed, with your arms at your sides. Slowly circle your right shoulder backwards. Repeat with your left shoulder, and continue on alternate sides.
- Place your right hand on your right shoulder. Move your elbow forwards, up, and back, in a circle. Repeat with your left elbow, and continue on alternate sides.
- Start with your arms straight at your sides. Keep your hips facing forwards, and move your right arm forward, up, and back, to form a large circle. Repeat on the left, and continue on alternate sides.
  Any of these arm circles can be done with both arms together.

Forward Bending: This is to stretch the muscles in your shoulders, trunk, and legs.

- Stand tall and relaxed. Stretching through your whole body, reach up towards the ceiling with your fingertips. Then, letting yourself bend at the hips and the knees, slowly bring your hands down towards the floor as far as is comfortable. Straighten up, and repeat.

Side Bending: This is to stretch the muscles in your sides and help keep your spine flexible.

- Stand tall and relaxed, with your feet apart and hands at your sides. Slowly bend to the left and right alternately, allowing your hands to slide down the sides of your legs. Stand tall in-between bends. Keep your legs straight. Make sure you are bending to the side and not letting your shoulders drop forwards. Move only as far as you can comfortably, and return to the upright position. Don't bounce into the movement.

Leg Swinging: This is to keep your hips mobile and to stretch the thigh muscles.

- Stand tall and relaxed, with your weight on your left leg. Rest your left hand on the back of a chair for support if necessary. Now swing your right leg forwards and backwards in a relaxed pendulum action. Gradually take your leg as high as you comfortably can, keeping your body fairly upright and letting your right knee bend. Repeat with your left leg.

Calf Stretching: This is to stretch your calves and keep your ankles mobile.

- Stand facing a wall at arm's length from it. Place your hands on the wall for support, and stretch your right leg out straight behind you, with the ball of your foot on the floor and your toes pointing towards the wall. Gently push your right heel towards the floor, allowing your left leg to bend as necessary.

Ankle Reaching: This is to stretch your lower back and the backs of your thighs.

- Sit on the floor, with your legs straight in front of you and your knees as near to the floor as is comfortable. Place your hands on top of your thighs. Slowly and smoothly slide your hands down your legs as far as you can comfortably reach. Return to the upright position, and repeat. Do not bounce into the movement.

Venturing Out

Swimming: This is good for increasing strength, stamina, and suppleness. It is particulary good if you are heavy or have some disability, as your body is supported by the water and there is no strain on your joints. Many local swimming pools have special sessions for women only or women with toddlers. There are often cheap rates, or you can buy a season ticket. Get in touch with your local authority leisure department.

Susan

Susan had always been heavy, but after the birth of her child her eating pattern became chaotic, and her weight increased. She had always been quite active, but as she became more ashamed of her body, she went out less. When it was suggested to her that she take up swimming, she was very reluctant. She said she would be ashamed to take her clothes off in public. However, she went to see what was available at her local swimming pool and leisure centre. They did not have sessions for women only, but they did have early-morning sessions, so she decided to go to these first thing and wear a long T-shirt over her bathing costume. She found that, at that time of day, most people at the pool were sleepy and preoccupied and did not notice her. She was thus able to go three times a week before her husband left for work.

Margaret

Margaret had always been in the top half of the normal range of weight. Diabetes ran in her family, and during her pregnancy she became mildly diabetic. After the birth of her child it disappeared. She was, however, concerned that if she did nothing about her weight, she would run a high risk of developing diabetes. She knew that she should exercise more. Her doctor had told her that swimming would be a good form of exercise. However, she felt that she would be unable to stretch her budget enough to visit the local swimming pool frequently, and so, with the help of her doctor, she started to mount a small campaign. Here is the letter she sent to the director of leisure at her local council, to the counsellors for her area, to the managers of the swimming pools, to her local MP, and to the Secretaries of State for Health and Social Services:

Dear ......,

I have a problem with my weight, and it is putting my health at risk. In the 1992 Government White Paper, Health of the Nation, one of the target areas is to reduce obesity within the UK. Exercise is recognised as being a good way of promoting health and for getting control over weight, and the Health Education Council has written a pamphlet suggesting that we do more exercise.

I would therefore like to go swimming, the form of exercise recommended by my doctor for me. There are, however, two problems that prevent me from doing this:

1. I cannot afford to go swimming on a regular basis.
2. I am frightened and intimidated when I do go.

*Is it not possible to have free swimming for those who are unable
to pay and whom doctors recommend a change in their lifestyle?*

*Also, would it be possible to have special sessions dedicated to
people like me, who are overweight or who have some other form of
disability?*

*I would be prepared to come and discuss this with you if
necessary.*

Thank you for your help

Margaret Miller

Once you have become more active, you may want to diversify your
exercise programme.

Cycling: This is good for stamina and leg strength. It is possible to get
second-hand bikes, and they are easy to maintain. You can cycle safely
in local parks or join a club.

Jogging and Running: This is popular, but you can develop overuse
injury to your lower limbs, so try to run on soft surfaces and with good
shoes. You can join clubs, and these do not only cater for high performers.

Golf: Some local authorities have public courses that are reasonably
priced.

Bowling: This is a sociable sport, and clubs are growing with recruits
of all ages.

Racket Sports: Some, like badminton, are good for beginners and can
be played at evening classes or local clubs.

Weight Training: More and more women are entering into this, but
you should learn how to do it safely by joining a class at your local leisure
centre.

Martial Arts and Judo: Many clubs are available, but make sure that
they belong to the national governing body.

Exercise Classes (Yoga, Movement and Dance): Make sure that the
class is at the right level. Start off with a beginners' class. It is important
that you get on with the teacher—not everybody will—so you may need
to change classes.

FURTHER READING

Bovey, S. (1989). *Being fat is not a sin*. London: Pandora.

Donald, C. (1987). *The fat woman measures up*. Charlottetown, Canada: Rageweed Press.

Harper, A., & Lewis, G. (1982). *The big beauty book*. New York: Holt, Reinhart & Winston.

Lyons, P., & Burgard, D. (1990). *Great shape: First fitness guide for large women*. Palo Alto, CA: Bull Publishing Co.

Nichols, G. (1984). *The fat black woman's poems*. London: Virago

Olds, R. (1984). *Big & beautiful*. Washington, DC: Acropolis Books

Palmer, A. (1985). *You fat slob*. London: Futura.

Roberts, N. (1985). *Breaking all the rules*. New York: Viking.

Weldon, F. (1982). *The fat woman's joke*. London: Hodder & Stoughton.

Wersba, B. (1987). *Fat: A love story*. London: Bodley Head.

CHAPTER EIGHT

Relapse: Walking In Circles—Or Not

Your eating disorder will remain your Achilles' Heel for the rest of your life, and it will be there to trip you up when you least expect it. You need to know how to prevent slips from occurring and what to do if a slip occurs.

PREVENTING SLIPS FROM OCCURRING

Plan Your Own Relapse

Every single person recovering from an eating disorder has to face numerous set-backs before the eating problem fades into the background. Knowing this can help you not to panic too much about the prospect of having a slip. Many sufferers find, once they haven't binged and vomited for a while, that they get increasingly panicky and worried that a set-back might strike any day now and might hit them harder then ever (Do you recognise this as an irrational belief ? You will find more on this subject in chapter 10). One practical way of dealing with this panic is to have a planned relapse. No, we are not having you on: bringing on, deliberately, what you fear most is an excellent way of getting on top of your fears.

- Set aside some time, buy your favourite binge foods, and have a binge. Spread all the food out on the table, and eat as much of it as you can. Concentrate on your binge as fully as you can. Can you bring yourself to stuff it down as you always used to? Can you bring yourself to eat similar amounts as you always used to? How does it feel? Is it really the worst thing that could ever happen to you? Having done this, do you feel you are back to square one?

- Repeat this exercise at least once a month if you are worried that you are doing too well.

WHAT TO DO IF A SLIP OCCURS

Don't make a mountain out of a molehill. Don't damn yourself. After you have slipped, your automatic thoughts will be to "awfulise" the event and to damn yourself. You may believe that if you slip once, you are a total failure and will never be able to get better. You may tell yourself that changing is too hard, and the discomfort of trying and failing and trying again is too much to bear.

It is important for you to try to argue yourself out of the illogicality of these statements. Consider the temptation to binge and vomit as a trial. You win some, and you lose some. One loss does not mean that you will fail next time.

Learning from Slips

Try to stand back from how you feel about your lapse, and take a cool critical look at how it actually came about. Don't say it just happened. There is always a reason. Ask yourself the following questions:

- Have you gone against any of the dietary ground-rules outlined in chapter 3? Have you allowed yourself to eat enough at mealtimes? Have you omitted meals or left long gaps between them?
- Is bingeing still the easiest and quickest way of getting pleasure in your life? If so, you will need to change your life so that there are other ways of getting pleasure that do not lead to long-term problems.
- Was your lapse caused by stress, upset, unhappiness, anxiety, or any other unpleasant feeling? If so, what other ways of dealing with these triggers do you have?

The more carefully you think about your lapse, the more it can teach you and can help you to make different plans, either to stop getting tempted or to cope differently if temptation arises. Don't just ignore a slip and rely on your willpower to change. Take active steps to change the behaviour and situations that act as triggers, and get others to help make these changes. If you do slip once, you can still decide whether you are going to continue to binge eat and have a complete relapse or whether you are going to stop the episode.

A WOMAN'S WORK IS NEVER DONE—OR IS IT?

Many women, and especially women with an eating disorder, devote the majority of their time to caring for other people's needs, whether at work, within the family, or within their social network, and they have difficulties looking after their own needs, or even recognising that they have needs and wants. An imbalance between shoulds, those activities that you see as chores or things you feel obliged to do, and "wants", those activities carried out for pleasure, is often responsible for relapse. "Shoulds" and "wants" are subjective, depending on pressures and circumstances. Table 8.1 shows the diary of one of our patients, Isabel, a young solicitor.

You can see that most of Isabel's day was made up of "shoulds". The only "wants" she allowed into her day were food-related, and these were all concentrated at the end of the day. Do you recognise this? Does food, when you allow yourself to have it, give you this much of a thrill? Often women with eating disorders find it difficult to give up overeating, as this constitutes the only thrill or pleasure in their life (and the one pleasure that is most easily accessible).

- Draw up your own "shoulds" and "wants" diary for a week.
- Are you the sort of person who allows the "shoulds" to take over your life? You need to create a balance in your life and to ensure that you

TABLE 8.1
Isabel's "shoulds" and "wants" Diary

Activity	Should	Want
Get up	+	
Drive to work	+	
Deal with mail & phone calls	+	
3 appointments	+	
Running late, no time for lunch	+	
Go to bank	+	
Writing reports	+	
2 further clients	+	
Shop—buy biscuits & chocolate to eat in the car		+ +
Drive home	+	
Make self sick		+
Tidy flat	+	
Iron clothes	+	
Finish reports for work	+	
Supper		+
Binge		+

incorporate into it activities in which you look after yourself—both your mind and body.

- How could you make sure there is more balance in your life?
- What could you do to comfort and excite yourself, besides eating?
- Make a list of your "wants" and desires. Include big and small things on your list: wild, decadent dreams like "a three-week holiday in a luxury hotel in Barbados", and some simple things, like "ten minutes to myself every morning to do some relaxation". Make a start with the small things, and make sure you incorporate at least one of those into every day.

CHAPTER NINE

The Wounds
of Childhood

Some of you will have been deprived of the safe, consistent loving and nurturing experience every child deserves. Problematic or inadequate parenting, with repeated arguments and violence amongst parents, physical abuse, and sexual abuse is common for sufferers of eating disorders. This can be the result of the parents splitting up or a parent dying, or it may stem from psychological problems in a parent, like depression or alcohol abuse.

In other cases the problems are less overt. Your parents may have had little time or energy for you, or they may have lacked interest in you, being physically or emotionally unavailable to you, perhaps because they were too preoccupied with their work or perhaps because they were depressed following the breakdown of their marriage. Or maybe they gave you the feeling that you would only be accepted if you were good, successful, or clever. Lack of approval and withheld affection can leave profound scars, with later difficulties in relationships.

Sandra

Sandra grew up in South Africa. Her parents split up when she was four. Her mother then remarried. The stepfather drank heavily. When he was drunk, he would beat Sandra and her two sisters or force them to drink whisky. There were incessant arguments between him and their mother. Sandra repeatedly witnessed her stepfather beating her mother. "We were terrified when they fought. I often feared he might kill my mother." Most of the time Sandra was left completely to her own devices. The family had several servants, one of whom forced Sandra to have sexual intercourse with him on several occasions. He threatened to kill her should she tell her parents. When Sandra was 12 years of age, her mother left the stepfather, and Sandra was sent to England to live with her natural father. "At first I wanted to live with him. In fact, when I still lived with my mother and stepfather I often dreamt that my father would come and rescue me. But once I was living with him, our relationship became quite fraught. He was pretty strict and tried to make me work for school. He often criticized me, the way I dressed, and my friends; he felt that I didn't work hard enough at school. I think he probably tried his best to get on with me, but I was pretty rebellious in my early teens, and I simply didn't trust him enough."

Such negative childhood experiences often produce low self-esteem, depression, suppressed anger, or open rebellion and difficulties in developing trusting relationships. Instead of adopting a "give-and-take" middle ground in your relationships, you may find yourself fluctuating between extreme positions where you either idealise people, putting them on a pedestal, or feel totally negative about them. This leads to loneliness or feeling let down or ignoring your own needs.

Do you recognise the following?

- Did you have to fend for yourself as your parents were absent or preoccupied; did you therefore have to grow up before your time?
- Were you ruled with an iron rod, with fear of violence to yourself or to others?—You may have been left feeling crushed or rebellious.
- Did you only feel loved if you came up to certain standards in looks, behaviour, or achievement?
- Do you feel that your parents were perfect? Were you and your parents best friends?—This may make it difficult for you to reach out and explore other relationships.
- Do you feel that you were envied? Did you have better chances than others?—This may make you deny and spoil your luck.
- Do you feel that your physical and emotional needs were neglected or damaged? Were you used as a scapegoat for your parents' feelings of anger or dissatisfaction?
- Draw your family tree.
- What are your memories of your early family life? Perhaps you can jot some things down. For example, how did your family deal with:
  - relatives
  - mealtimes/celebrations

- school/friends
- religion/authority figures
- money/talents/gifts
- illness/losses
- Write your life story, and put in events as suggested above, but also identify the abstract beliefs and motivations that underlay these events. Show your story to a friend.

SEXUAL ABUSE

Sexual abuse in childhood is a form of trauma that may be particularly difficult to come to terms with because of the aura of secrecy and taboo that surrounds it.

What is Sexual Abuse?

Child sexual abuse happens when an adult or older person touches or uses a child in a sexual way. This can include many different kinds of activities but the main thing is that, by being bigger, stronger, or having power or authority in the victim's life, the adult can trap, lure, force, or bribe them into sexual activity.

How Do I Know if I Have Been Sexually Abused?

Here are some examples of the different things that can happen:

Being ...

- cuddled or kissed in a way that left you feeling uncomfortable
- bathed in a way that made you feel uneasy
- made to watch sexual acts or look at other people's genitals
- shown sexual films or videos, or being forced to listen to sexual talk
- made to pose for "sexual" photographs
- touched on your breasts or genitals
- made to touch an adult's or older person's genitals
- made to have oral sex
- penetrated (having the adult thrust a finger, his penis, or an object inside the vagina or anus)
- raped (penetrated using force or violence)

There are other, less obvious things that may have been done or said to you that you have found abusive.

Why is it Wrong?

This form of early sexual activity is wrong because it hurts the victim, sometimes physically, but more often psychologically. We know that it can cause confusion, fear, anger, shame, self-blame and leave the victim with a very poor opinion of themselves. Without help, the victim can sometimes have serious problems in later life.

It is wrong because everybody should have a right to decide what happens to their body. Adults should normally protect that right for children and young people, so any situation where physical force is used or threatened, or where the person feels they can't say no, can be called sexual assault. Children and young people, for many reasons, can't really say no to adults, nor have they the power to stop them. Young children do not even understand what is happening. The adult in this situation is always committing a crime. About 10% of women in the community and approximately 30 to 40% of women with eating disorders have been sexually abused in their childhood or raped in later life. The spectrum of abuse ranges from one-off experiences to repeated abuse over years. Any form of sexual abuse constitutes a gross exploitation of a power relationship. Often the abuser is a member of the family or someone known to the family.

TRYING TO MAKE SENSE OF IT

Victims of sexual abuse commonly feel that they are to blame for what happened, that they allowed the abuse to happen or somehow provoked it. Physical force or psychological threats are often used to silence the victim and are designed to confuse you by making you feel as though you are in the wrong or as if you invited the advances. It is also common for a victim who is brave enough to discuss the abuse, to meet with disbelief, and the whole thing getting hushed up in the family. In many cases the perpetrator goes on living within the family or near-by.

Hazel

Hazel was sexually abused for a number of years by her father's brother, from when she was very young. She would often spend summer holidays with this uncle and his wife. "When my aunt was out doing the shopping, he would often ask me whether I wanted him to read a story. He then took me on his lap and began to touch me up, my genitals, my breasts. I could feel that he had an erection. I had a sense that this was wrong. I didn't ask him to stop. I didn't tell my parents at the time." Hazel eventually mustered up the courage to tell her parents about this when she was 16. "My mother was very good about it, but my father, I think, still doesn't believe me. He accused me of lying and got very cross with me. I think he was totally shocked that something like this could happen in his family. I never now go to see my uncle. My parents still go, because they wouldn't want open conflict in the family. I am really frightened that he could do it to someone else, too."

Many victims of sexual abuse feel that the abuse completely changed the way they feel about themselves as a person and that they have been left with a wound that will never heal. Kathy, another one of our patients, whose father repeatedly raped her when she was in her teens, said, "it feels like some poison is growing inside me".

- If you have been sexually abused it may seem too difficult to talk to someone about this at the moment—or you might decide you want to do something about it now.
- First, it will help if you read other sufferers' experiences of abuse. You will not feel so alone, full of shame and different to the rest of society.

At the end of this chapter you will find a reading list that may be of interest to you. Go to your local library, and order one of the books.

- You may want to talk to someone anonymously about it. Self-help lines are available (unfortunately they are often busy).
- Write down what happened to you, but as a story of a court scene, as if it had happened to someone else. Write down what the prosecuting lawyer for the victim would say. Here is the way he might set about it:
  - How did the abuse start?
  - Were there ways the abuser got you to keep it secret?
  - How long did it continue?
  - What were the worst things about it?
  - What did the abuser do?
  - Write down what the defence lawyer for the perpetrator would say.
  - Then write down the jury's response, and finally, the judge's speech.
- Could you show your story to anyone else? They may be able to help complete the lawyer's case, give more of the jury's verdict, and ensure that the judge was wise. If the victim of the story was your own child, would any of the arguments differ?

Trying to understand and make sense of what happened to you leads to confusing feelings, so try to answer these questions:

- Do you blame yourself for the abuse? Who else is to blame?
- Do you have secret fears about yourself? Or about others?
- If you are angry, what are you angry about?
- If you are scared, what are you scared about?
- It gets particularly confusing if you have some good memories and feelings about the abuser. This doesn't indicate that you are a monster. Children naturally try to see the good in things. What were the good memories? Do you have good memories you want to keep?
- Similarly, many victims are left with mixed feelings about their parents. What are your good and bad feelings towards your parents?

- Rank the strength of your feelings on a scale of 1 to 10.
- Draw yourself and other members of the family. See how you draw them and what feelings these drawings evoke in you.
- Record your feelings in your diary, and do the ABC detective work as outlined in chapter 2.

The Right to be Angry

Anger is a natural response to abuse, but you may have learnt that getting angry leads to more abuse, or you may feel that anger is not what you are allowed to feel. You may have witnessed terrible violence done in anger and so think that it is necessary to suppress it.

The abuser often stifles or deflects the victim's anger and it is turned inwards, therefore you feel bad or you take your anger out on yourself by hurting yourself or deadening your anger with food. Is it fair to continue to add to the burden of hurt and pain carried by the child victim inside you?

What Can You Do with Angry Feelings?

The first step is to recognise your anger and allow yourself a glimpse at it. You may need to spend 15 minutes quietly meditating, focusing on your anger. Listen to your body and its sensations. Give it time, and you may be able to answer all of the questions below.

- Who are you angry with?—The abuser? Your parent? Yourself? The world?
- Are you just annoyed or are you furious?
- Look at what you normally do with angry feelings:
  - Do you yell at people?
  - Do you tease and criticise?
  - Do you lash out?
  - Do you break things?
  - Do you hurt yourself?
  - Do you take your feelings out on someone else?
  - Do you keep them bottled up?
  - Do you tell people about them?
  - Do you do something to change what is making you angry?
  - Do you remain passive?
  - What have you done to express your anger in the past?
  - What would you like to do to show people that you are angry?
  - Do you ever secretly think about the things you would like to do to show your anger?

Here are some ways that have helped other people get their angry feelings about abuse out into the open. You might feel inhibited at first when you are trying them, but they often do work.

- Imagine a child you know or care about being treated in the same way you were treated.
- Read other victims' stories (see reading list)—perhaps you can feel angry for them.
- Go somewhere safe, and get into an angry posture—make angry faces, shout and swear, scream. Get a friend to scream with you!
- Try asking your supporter to sit in front of you and put up their palms facing you. Now push against them with your palms. Push hard. Get your supporter to push back. Get mad.
- Punch cushions. Hitting the bed with a tennis racket, or a rolled-up newspaper is just as good and makes a great noise.
- With your helper, act out situations which make you feel angry.

Make some rules about this—not hurting anyone else, not hurting yourself.

- Talk to your pillow/doll and explain why you are so angry. Sometimes venting your anger can make you aware of other kinds of feelings as a powerful aftermath—loneliness, sadness, and grief. It is a good idea to have someone around who understands what you are trying to do and can comfort you.

Here are some ideas for directly targeting your anger:

- Draw pictures of the abuser. Tell them what you would like to do to them. Tear them up into little pieces. Put them on the wall, and throw things at them.
- Make your own models of the abuser in clay or plasticine. Stick pins in them. Squash them. Break them into little pieces.
- Imagine the abuser in "the empty chair". If you can't say angry things to him, get your supporter to do it.
- Listen to family members, friends, or your helper being angry on your behalf.
- Make a list of the ways in which the abuse has affected you. You are bound to find things to be angry about.
- Write a letter to the person who abused you (even if the person is no longer around or even dead). You shouldn't send the letter. It is private—just for you. Write all your angry thoughts in it. Don't hold back. Call the abuser all the names you want. Describe how hurt you are and why.
- Try dictating the letter onto a tape-recorder.

- Re-read your letter, or play back your tape. Add some more before you put it somewhere safe.
- Or take out your letter, and rip it to shreds. Tear it into the smallest pieces possible.

Sometimes you can feel so much anger that is hard to talk without losing control. Try some physical exercise. Run, jog, take the dog for a walk. Try some aerobics. Jump up and down.

At some point or another you may have strong feelings of wanting to get back at the person who has hurt you. You dream of revenge—or even murder. Wanting revenge is a natural impulse, a sane response. Of course you can't act on it, but let yourself imagine it to your heart's content. That is one way of getting it out of your system.

Remember, being angry with someone doesn't cancel out the good feelings you might have about them. You have a right to your anger. Expressing it clears the way for you to feel whole again.

GRAPPLE WITH GUILT AND SELF-BLAME

Many victims of abuse are plagued by the thought that they are to blame for what happened. You may be aware that part of you enjoyed what happened, or that you are to blame because you accepted bribes, or that simply by going along with the abuse you are somehow responsible for it.

NO, NEVER! No one has the right to abuse you sexually either by force or by abusing their position. It is never the victim's fault. The abuser is totally responsible for his own behaviour. It is never anything the victim does or says that causes the abuse. Equally, the victim is not responsible for what happens to the family or abuser after speaking out.

Do you torture yourself by telling yourself that:

- It was something about you that "invited" the abuse?
- You were the kind of person who "deserved" it?
- You enjoyed the special attention involved ... or the rewards ... or you accepted money?
- You "used" the secret to get some kind of advantage over the abuser?
- You experienced pleasurable physical feelings associated with the abuse?
- You didn't tell?
- You didn't do enough to stop the abuse?
- You didn't do enough to prevent brothers and sisters being abused?
- By telling, you have upset your family or brought them unwelcome attention?
- You are responsible for breaking up the family?
- You have brought punishment on the abuser?
- You have behaved in destructive or self-destructive ways?

Pretend your list belonged to someone else who has suffered abuse, and you were that person's friend. What would you say to them?

Often the abuse starts so early that you didn't know what was going on. Although you may have suspected that it wasn't quite right, by the time you knew that it was wrong it had been going on so long you felt you couldn't object or tell. Remember that children have to trust adults and can be confused easily, but always need affection and attention and so will join in any interaction with an adult. Sexual responses are instinctive and can develop at an early age.

WILL THE EFFECTS ALWAYS BE THERE?

Different people are affected in different ways, and the after-effects of the abuse don't just depend on what happened, but on what help and support the victim has. Often abuse leads to difficulties that persist in adult life and with relationships with others. Once you realise how your abuse affects you, you can overcome it.

REMEMBER: EVERY VICTIM CAN BE A SURVIVOR!

GET A TOEHOLD ONTO TRUST

After abuse of any sort, lack of trust is imprinted on your personality. When you can't trust, a vicious circle begins. The less you trust, the fewer friends you will have and the more isolated you become. You do not give yourself the opportunity to relearn that people can be trusted, you feel lonely and vulnerable and guard yourself more.

Going through life without trust is very lonely, so when you have the courage to try, take it slowly. You may have setbacks, but don't give up, the gains are great. You may find it helpful to read *The Little Prince* by Antoine De St. Exupery, who recognised that love involved the risk of being hurt but that a life bereft of friendships was no life. Trust will take time to develop—be patient. Eventually you will experience its components—honesty, acceptance, and respect. Beware of romantic myths, such as those portrayed in Mills & Boon novels, suggesting that there is only one man to be with in your life, or that a "Prince Charming" (strong, macho) will whisk you off your feet (in real life he may turn out to be a domineering brute).

It is often difficult to get the balance between caring and dependence right when you have not experienced such balance in your childhood. You may need to spend longer in the phase of developing friendships with women before you start relationships with men. It is better that you do make this work thoroughly, rather than risk entering into another victim/abuser relationship. Try to answer the following questions:

- Do you feel that, if you depend on someone, they are in charge, and you have to give in?
- Do you fear that getting close to someone will end up with you being hurt, and therefore you opt for the "lonely but in charge" road?
- Do you swing between feeling of contempt for others and the idea that they will ridicule or humiliate you?
- Do you swing between feeling a brute or a baby?

If any of these patterns ring true, go back to your family tree and family diagram.

- What are your family mottoes? Where do these myths come from?
- Re-write the story in the same way as Roald Dahl rewrote fairy stories (*Revolting Rhymes*). How can you change the ending? Can you make people act out of character and break the myth? Can you write a triumphant ending, or add humour to it? Start with "Once upon a time there was a little child." Plan to show your stories to a friend.

COMING TO TERMS

Unfortunately, you cannot re-write the past, no matter how painful it was, no matter how hurt and wronged you still feel. You can't undo the damage. You must learn to say goodbye to the "wish" for better parents and continue with the rest of your life. Banishing the longing for what might have been will enable you to make room for what can be and the "real" people in your life, even if they are not perfect.

To help you come to terms with the past and to understand how this colours present relationships, you may decide you want counselling. Some contact addresses of counselling agencies are given at the end of the book.

FURTHER READING

Angelou, M. (1984). *I know why the caged bird sings*. London: Virago.

Bass, E., & Thornton, L. (1983). *I never told anyone*. New York: Harper & Row.

Morris, M. (1982). *If I should die before I wake*. New York: Black Swan.

Spring, J. (1991). *Cry hard and swim. The story of an incest survivor.* London: Virago.

The four books above are written by people who have personally experienced sexual abuse.

Bain, O., & Saunders, M. (1990). *Out in the open: A guide for young people who have been sexually abused.* London: Virago Upstarts. This book was specifically written for sexually abused teenagers discussing what happens once the truth is out.

Gallagher, V. (1991). *Becoming whole again. Help for women survivors of childhood sexual abuse.* Blue Ridge Summit, PA: TAB Books.

Stones, R. (1987). *Too close encounters and what to do about them.* London: Magnet

CHAPTER TEN

Food for Thought

We all have ideas of how the world and people in it work, even if most of the time these are unconscious. A lot of these ideas stem from childhood (i.e. if your parents always told you that you are a nice and worthwhile person, it is likely you will think of yourself as nice and worthwhile, whereas if they told you that you are fat and selfish, it is very likely you will grow up thinking you are fat and selfish). On the basis of these ideas we try to understand what goes on around us ("even though I have made a few mistakes, my friends will go on liking me because they like me for what I am" or "people won't like me unless I am perfect" or "unless I please people, they will guess how selfish I am"). We also use our ideas to predict what the likely outcome of events will be ("that nice boy who asked me out will probably never do so again as I am so stupid and ugly"). Problems arise when a person's set of ideas is not continually updated in the light of new experiences and a person gets stuck with a number of beliefs and ways of coping learnt as a child, but which are false or inappropriate. Sufferers of eating disorders usually have many self-defeating beliefs about themselves and the world at large. Often these come from difficult childhood experiences. In other cases the eating disorder itself makes the person feel that they are hopeless, disgusting, a mess, stupid, or worthless. Many of the irrational thoughts are focused on, and fuelled by, the eating symptoms (e.g. "I have binged again/ I've been unable to eat enough again, I am a truly worthless person"), others centre on life in general (e.g. "my boyfriend left me, I am so unattractive, I will never find another man again").

TOAD IN A HOLE

Often sufferers of eating disorders have been indoctrinated from childhood to believe that they were not quite right.

Joy

Joy had felt low about herself for years, and as a teenager she had taken several overdoses and cut herself. She confessed that she had never felt liked and cared for as a child. She noticed that there were many photographs of her brother and sister around the house, but there were none of her. It was a family joke that she had been a very ugly baby and child. Her mother had a friend who had a daughter two months older than Joy. Throughout her life Joy had been negatively compared to the friend's daughter. She was ridiculed and humiliated because she was the ugly, chubby one. The two families spent all their time together, and Joy could never get away from being put down.

As in Joy's case, there may have been powerful family myths built up around you (not clever enough, not pretty enough, not ...). The scars of being the family's ugly duckling can last for a long time.

Jameela

Jameela's father was from India and her mother from Ireland. She grew up in a small village in the South East of England. "I had a lot of trouble at school. I was often teased because of my exotic looks and somehow grew up thinking that my differentness meant I was defective in some way. Even now, whenever the slightest thing goes

A TOAD IN THE HOLE

wrong, I tell myself over and over how worthless I am." This led to her avoiding social contact. Because she felt defective, she didn't know what to say or how to interact, and so she appeared unfriendly, standoffish, and aloof and was left alone.

Do any of these ring true for you?

- I don't know what to say when I'm with others, I therefore avoid social meetings of any sort.
- I lack confidence, I think that people won't like me, will criticise me, or will find me stupid.
- I fear that if I speak it will come out wrong, and people will laugh.

These self-defeating thoughts often go round continuously in a person's head, nagging and undermining, wearing a person out, intensifying if the slightest thing goes wrong. Worse still, they actually make things go wrong. Say, for example, you expect other people not to like you. You therefore behave as if they didn't like you by being withdrawn and defensive. It is, then, likely that other people will treat you as if something was wrong with you. This will strengthen your belief that people don't like you. This is what's called a self-fulfilling prophecy.

Self-defeating thoughts are the root of depression and low self-esteem, and they make eating problems worse. It is, therefore, very important to try to become aware of these thoughts/beliefs and to question them.

THE GLOOM-AND-DOOM SCENARIO
A sense of helplessness, hopelessness, and inevitability is often the result of irrational thoughts that combine three elements: (1) you shouldering the responsibility when things go wrong ("I let her down"); (2) thinking that things will be the same forever ("I ALWAYS let her down"); and (3) things will be the same wherever you go ("I always let EVERYBODY down"—in other words, the feeling that failures are due to your own doing or personality, and that this will always be the case in all situations. This is a really paralysing attitude to have because it makes you feel you have no control over events and can't change anything or that the events over which you do have some control will inevitably turn out bad. Ultimately this leads to depression.

ISN'T LIFE DREADFUL?
Are you one of the people for whom life is dreadful? Just one catastrophe, disaster, major flop after another? Maybe you are truly unlucky—there are some people who seem to attract problems, but if everything always seems to go wrong, especially for you, maybe it is something to do with your attitudes rather than how things really are.

Gina

Gina always went around thinking the worst things only happened to her. Her mother was very bitter about having been left by Gina's father when Gina was little and had always talked about how hard and unfair life was. "I suppose I somehow learnt to see things through her eyes, to always concentrate on the negative side of things. Everything was an insurmountable hurdle put in my path to trip me up. And I'd let it trip me up. In some ways I draw some weird sort of satisfaction from things being difficult for me. My husband is just the opposite—difficulties are there to be overcome."

WRACKED BY GUILT?

A powerful sense of having done something wrong accompanies many sufferers of eating disorders in their daily life. Guilty thoughts may be especially strong after eating. "I reached the point where, even after eating a bunch of grapes, I'd feel totally guilty, like I'd committed a major crime. I'd know it's total nonsense and yet I'd have these pangs of guilt." Guilt is a hard problem to tackle.

- Try to imagine a court-room scenario, with the judge shouting out, "The accused has been found guilty of eating a bunch of grapes (or whatever it is you feel guilty of—eating 5 cream buns ... not being sympathetic to her friend's problems at all times ... not visiting her parents often enough). She will be sentenced to 5 years' hard labour."
- How might a brilliant defense lawyer tackle the accusation against you and sway the jury in your favour? He might say, "What has the accused actually done wrong? Since when is it a crime in this country to eat a bunch of grapes? I admit to eating a bunch of grapes only this

morning. Is there anyone in this courtroom who has never eaten grapes?"

PLEASE, PLEASE THEM

Some people feel under a constant obligation to others. They have a central feeling that they will only be loved on condition that they are worthy, clever, charming, or attractive enough. Sheila MacLeod, in her book, *The Art of Starvation* (1981, London: Virago), describes this. "The anorexic is behaving like a person who has never experienced mother-love. She is behaving as if the world were full of fathers only, fathers who have to be impressed, pleased or gratified." And, of course, the same is true for many sufferers of bulimia.

The Plastic Pleaser

John

John had been sensitive as a child; he was aware how distressed his mother was when he and his brothers came in dirty and made a mess in the house she took pains to keep clean. He couldn't bear her cold silences, which accompanied her anger. Homesick at boarding-school, he felt it was his duty to cope. It was difficult to steer a safe course between punishment with severe beatings from the teachers for failing to come up to standard and bullying from other boys for being a swot or goody-goody. He became highly skilled at aiming to please.

Like John,

- Do you fear not pleasing others, because you might fail to get love or approval or be criticised or abused?
- Do you please others regardless of how you feel, suppress your own feelings, try to understand how others tick so you can maintain their goodwill?
- Are you unable to say no and take on too much in order not to let others down, or put things off because you can't bear to get it wrong?
- Do you keep feelings bottled up because they signal inner needs?

- Are you concerned that you may dissolve into tears or explode into anger if you let anything out?
- Are you frightened of being ridiculed or considered as wet or a wimp?

If any of these seem true, can you think of any situations from the past that could explain things? When you recognise that you are falling into the pleasing pit, stop yourself and try to think how your behaviour is affecting others:

- If you never let people know what you really want or feel, they are left trying to read your mind and divine your wishes. Of course they will get it wrong at times, which gives them a profound sense of failure and deprives them of the pleasure of pleasing you. They may perceive you as being superior and aloof.
- If you aim to say and do everything to give in to others, they will think of you as spineless, characterless, without individuality; they are bound to find you uninteresting.
- If you always try to please, you will get angry and frustrated if your efforts are not noticed, and it is impossible not to let this show, even in subtle ways.
- Being a silent martyr can be intensely irritating, as it presumes that you are right and does not give you any opportunity to see the other person's side of things.
- Aiming to please may be a selfish wish, as it may involve taking the moral high ground, but it also deprives everyone else of the chance to give and to be nice.

The Shrew Untamed

Some people take the opposite stand to pleasing/placation as their way of coping and refuse to meet the demands made by others: "If I must—I won't." Often these two coping styles coexist in the same person, who may be all charm and helpfulness to acquaintances and yet appear stubborn and unyielding to members of the family.

- Do you feel caged and restricted if obliged to do things?
- How does this make you feel? Furious, frightened, or defiant?
- Does this refusal mean that you can't reach your full potential?

John shifted between these two poles. Most of the time he did what others wanted, but armed with the cloak of his bulimia nervosa, he was able to make a stand and refuse to do things.

How to Struggle out of the Pleasing Pit

Your aim with both of these two modes of coping is to strike a balance between looking after your needs—i.e. trying to ensure that things are good enough for you—and doing what will please others. Initially it may be difficult for you to establish what you want—you may need to tackle this using a formalised problem-solving approach (see chapter 2). Once you have thought of some alternative ways of behaving, you can write a balance sheet, which will help you define what seems best for you. Once you have established your goals, you may need to use assertiveness skills to claim them (see chapter 11).

Remember to chant these battle-cries to give yourself strength:

- You cannot please everyone all of the time!
- You cannot love or be loved by everyone!
- Sticking up for yourself is not selfish!

THE DICTATORSHIP OF CONTROL

A common way in which people with eating disorders organise their thinking is to aim for total control as there is an underlying fear of chaos.

Linda

Linda kept the flat in which she lived in perfect order. Each evening she would spend an hour cleaning the bathroom and kitchen. Her flatmates did not see this as an indirect message for them to work hard to keep the flat clean. Rather, they saw this behaviour as boring and unpleasantly intrusive into their lives. They avoided Linda whenever possible and joked about their "little housewife" flatmate behind her back. As soon as possible they said they were leaving. At work, her need for control and order led her repeatedly to check on the people with whom she worked to ensure that they were doing what she asked. She would attempt to delegate some organisational task but would later do the job herself, sending letters that overrode the decisions made by her colleagues. Her workmates found this intolerable; they shunned her at social occasions and laughed at her once she had left the room. A further way that Linda controlled her life was to control her eating and exercise habits.

Under my thumb....

- Like Linda, do you have to clean or check on things obsessively or keep things in perfect order at all times?
- Sit and try to image in detail what you fear might happen if you fail to come up to your standards. Close your eyes, and conjure up the situation. Play through it slowly. What would you do, how could you cope? Imagine a friend of yours whom you admire as strong. How would they cope, what would they think and do? Is a critical inner voice trying to sabotage you? Tell your critic that no matter what happens you will either find a way of coping, or enlist help.
- Plan to experiment gradually by giving up one aspect of control. This might mean relaxing some control over your dietary rules. Or perhaps you will deliberately leave some housework undone, e.g. delay the washing-up by 10 minutes. Observe the anxiety and guilt that will overcome you, and see how long they last. If you survive your small experiment successfully, you may be ready to relinquish excessive control in the next area. You must practice challenging your excessive standards every day in little ways.

Here are some arguments that may come in useful when you are trying to tackle this type of thinking trap:

- I cannot control fate—life will throw up events without any justice.
- Although I can do some things to stack the dice of life in my favour, luck also plays a role.
- Learning to tolerate a bit of mess and chaos is an important survival skill.

The Ace of Asceticism

Another way in which the craving for control may show itself is to restrict our own instinctive drives. This may lead to the feeling that it is wrong to have our own wishes or needs met. If we do acknowledge our need for comfort, we feel guilty or lacking in moral fibre. If we do get what we want, we are sickened by our selfishness or childishness.

Victoria

Victoria was the youngest daughter of a Kenyan businessman. Her father was very successful, which meant that he and her mother were busy and often out in the evenings for business reasons. It always seemed an imposition to Victoria to ask for help with homework or to chat about school. Victoria felt her parents were too busy to be interested in her; she had to cope. She felt very different and isolated from the other girls at school, as she was the only African in her class. She had no want for material things. Her father bought her a flat when she was 15 and arranged for this to be rented out. From the age of 15 onwards, her father's business concerns took him and his wife back to Kenya for five months every year. Victoria was left in the charge of her sister, who was one year older but who had a close relationship with a boyfriend. She came to us with an eating disorder, crying for no reason, and with a pervasive sense of loneliness.

- Like Victoria, you may describe your parents in glowing terms as they may have provided you with every material comfort, but they may have neglected your emotional development and the need to give sufficient time, support, and attention to you.
- Like Victoria, you may feel it is ridiculous to feel like a deprived baby with distress that you cannot define when your parents treat you as an adult. Somehow, however, the silver spoon jars against your teeth.
- Your parents may do the opposite and make you run short materially to "strengthen you". You then feel furious but can't explain or admit it when they pay more for vet's fees for the cat, than they do on helping you start at university.
- Alternatively, the neediness inside may drive you to use or fantasise about other forms of comfort—eating, taking drugs, spending money, or sexual relationships. Because you do not understand what underlies this need for comfort and care, it seems like greed.

The Patina of Power

The same underlying mechanisms can lead to the drive to create superwoman who can be best and tackle anything. The compulsive perfectionist strives for bigger and better without reflecting on the need or the appropriateness of the goal. Trying to give your best, if you can, is not a bad thing and will be helpful to you in many walks of life. However, people with eating problems often have unrealistically high expectations of themselves and the world—they don't just try to do their best, they have to succeed at being best at all times; everything has got to be flawless and just so. This can include their personal appearance, their work, and their interpersonal relationships.

Ask yourself the following questions: Why do you need such success? Why have you got to outsmart or outshine others? Why do you need to compete so hard?

Maybe your drive for perfectionism is the result of an underlying fear that nobody will like you unless you are superwoman and that errors, mistakes, sloppiness, oversights, and carelessness are unforgivable. Or you may be frightened of chaos, or are lonely and lost without a goal. Often a less-than-perfect performance makes the person think that they are totally useless, but boy, how exhausting it is trying to be perfect! Not just that—perfectionism strangles the messy, lively, spontaneous, creative side of your personality.

Society's approval of your striving for financial security or to be the best at your job may lull you into the belief that you do not have to question why you are so needy.

Emily

Emily became Personal Assistant to the Political Editor of a National Newspaper. "It was an incredibly ambitious, high-powered work environment." Emily did several hours' unpaid overtime every day to prove to her boss that she was excellent. "I tried to read his mind and do things he might ask me to do before he even asked. I wanted him to think that I was the best Personal Assistant he had ever had." However, she rarely got any praise, and one day she overheard her boss talking about her to someone else: "Oh yes Emily, my new P.A., she's trying awfully hard; her work is okay, but she's so tense, it rubs off on everyone else in the office." Emily was shattered. You can see that Emily's attempts to be perfect were fuelled by her need to please.

OVER TO YOU

Each time you feel inappropriately upset or act against your own interest, look for your thinking errors—thoughts that fuel your upset. One way to establish whether a belief is rational or irrational is to ask yourself the following questions:

• What and where is the evidence for that?
• What other explanations are there?
• What would you think about this belief if you were another person looking at yourself?
• Am I trying to please, to be perfect or be in control?

You need to identify the patterns of behaving, which serve you badly. It can be pretty difficult to "catch" your self-defeating thoughts in action, as they come on so quickly and automatically. You may find that your self-defeating thoughts come from one or several of the areas outlined above, or they may not fit neatly into any of the categories at all.

When you have recognised some of the thinking traps in your own life, start trying to notice them each time they happen and record them in your diary.

• In your diary, write down the "A's" (antecedents)—thoughts or feelings that happened just before you felt emotionally disturbed or behaved self-defeatingly—and find the "C's" (consequences)—disturbed feelings or self-defeating behaviour that resulted.

- Make two columns: In the first, put your self-defeating irrational belief, e.g."I must do well or I am totally useless." In the second, put a rational thought, e.g. "I'd prefer to do well but don't have to."

Table 10.1 lists examples of the irrational thoughts experienced by Emily, whom we introduced to you earlier, and the more rational thoughts she learnt to replace them with in treatment.

- To add to this method of challenging your self-defeating thoughts, it is useful to have strategies in which you change the consequences of these thoughts, not just by replacing them with more appropriate thoughts, but by what you do. Have a plan of action well thought out, so that you can use it the next time one of these self-defeating patterns emerges. For example, phone a friend, go and visit someone, go through the balance sheet, etc.

Below are some more of the argued responses to the different self-defeating thoughts shared by sufferers of eating disorders. Some are to do with eating, some are to do with other areas of life.

Eva: "It is irrational for me to be overwhelmed by guilt for having slightly more food than I think is right."
"I find it difficult to eat normally, but that doesn't mean it's impossible."
"When people refuse my invitations, it doesn't mean that I have done something wrong."
"Doing something foolish makes me a person who acts foolishly, not a total fool."
Jane: "I feel very good if I can keep my weight down. That doesn't prove that it is good for me to do this."
Val: "Even when I have a strong urge to eat, I don't have to."
Alison: "It is not awful to be disapproved of, only uncomfortable. I can always choose to accept myself, even when I do stupid acts."

TABLE 10.1
Emily's Self-defeating Thoughts and Counter-arguments

Irrational Thoughts	Rational Thoughts
If I am not outstanding in my work, people will see me as a totally insignificant person, who isn't worthwhile knowing.	That doesn't follow at all. There is much more of significance in a person than their performance at work. And besides, even if I am not outstanding, I can still do competent work.
To be worthwhile as a human being, I must be loved and approved of by everyone.	You can't rate a person by who loves or hates them.

"When I make a mistake, such as eating more than I feel I should, or get something wrong, this only proves that I am fallible and human."

Chantal: "With hard work, I am sure I can manage to eat more over the next few days. It will be great not to feel exhausted."

"Not knowing how this (important) project will turn out makes me anxious and concerned, but perhaps I can also use it to be a bit more curious and adventurous about things."

Tracey: "Falling back several times and losing weight is a challenge that may enable me to learn how to accept myself fully with all my fallibility and foolish behaviour."

"Having lost several jobs in a row may provide me with the challenge and determination to find and keep a suitable job."

SHAKE OFF SHAME

Feelings of shame, embarrassment, and humiliation are closely linked to the idea that you must be perfect or else nobody will like you. To beat these feelings, try to think of something you can do that you consider would be shameful, foolish, or ridiculous and that you would be particularly ashamed to do in public—not something like walking in the street naked, which would get you into real trouble, and not an act like slapping someone, which would hurt or bother other people—something you would really like to do but wouldn't have done or something merely foolish that you would not normally do. Think vividly of doing this act, and let yourself feel ashamed about it.

Go and do your "shameful act" in public, and while doing it work on your feelings so that you don't feel ashamed and embarrassed and humiliated, even though others may be laughing at you and thinking you're a fool for doing it. Plan to perform at least one "shameful" act each week. These are some ideas other patients have given:

- Wear an out-of-fashion suit or dress that is still serviceable.
- Don't wear any make-up, and go around with holes in your tights for a day.
- Dress comfortably for a formal affair.
- Tell a friend or relative about your eating disorder.
- Confess your inadequacies to significant people.
- Stuff balloons or cushions under your clothes, so that you seem to be much fatter than you are. Go around like this for a day.
- Go into the public changing room in a shop or a swimming bath, rather than into a single cubicle.
- Go to a joke shop or to a theatrical outfitters, and get something that will make you look as though your stomach or bottom is very big.
- Deliberately let a small thing go wrong at work.

FURTHER READING

Beck, A.T. (1976). *Cognitive therapy and the emotional disorder.* London: Penguin Books.

Blackburn, I.M. (1987). *Coping with depression.* Edinburgh: Chambers.

Burns, D, D. (1990). *The feeling good handbook.* New York: Penguin Group, USA (Plume).

Carter-Scott, C. (1988). *Negaholics. Overcome your lack of confidence. A twelve-step programme to recovery.* London: Century.

Palladino, C. D. (1989). *Developing self-esteem. A positive guide for personal success.* London: Kogan Page Ltd.

Wilde-McCormick, E. (1990). *Change for the better. A life-changing self-help psychotherapy programme.* London: Unwin Paperbacks.

CHAPTER ELEVEN

Finding Your Voice

Did you recognise yourself in the plastic pleaser or the subject of control or standards as described in chapter 10? Are you a person whose life is ruled and ruined by shoulds, drained by giving and giving and giving, until you feel totally tired out?

Do others take advantage of you because you will say "yes" to whatever they ask you, even if you would like to shout "no, no, no"? Are you unable to refuse any favours for fear of hurting the feelings of the other person irrevocably and beyond repair? Do you worry that, if you ever say what you want, you might be seen as totally self-obsessed and selfish?

If your answer is "yes" to any of these questions, read on. You suffer from lack of assertiveness! This is often the result of having extremely low self-esteem, feeling that you are totally insignificant or unloveable.

Sally

Sally is a case in point. She is a 20-year-old secretary in a small, successful company. "I feel nobody is really interested in me, I am not a very nice or interesting person to be with." When Sally came into treatment, she felt so bad about herself that she constantly had to pacify her feelings of guilt, shame, or self-disgust and prove her worth and usefulness by being everything to everybody, looking after others practically or emotionally. "We are four girls in the office. If our boss pops round the corner and says, "who is going to make us a cup of coffee, then?" it's always me who jumps up.

Needless to say, the washing-up is also left to me. The others just won't do it. I often stay behind to clear up when everybody has gone home." Sally also regularly took on twice as much work as everybody else. Once or twice her boss tried to be supportive to her by asking one of the other girls in the office to take some of Sally's load. "I didn't like that at all; I know he was only trying to be helpful, but I felt totally guilty afterwards." Is Sally a masochist or a martyr? Probably neither. However, she had got very used to letting herself be used as a doormat and found it very threatening not to be one. She feared that, if she gave up the role of a doormat, others would reject her.

Sometimes the fear of a lot of pent-up anger or frustration coming out is what stops a person from speaking their mind.

Cindy

Cindy, a 20-year-old student, shared a flat with another girl. "Although we are supposed to be equals in the flat, I don't seem to have the right to say what I think about things. Alison, my flatmate, is very outspoken and often really thoughtless. It's been irritating me for a while. The other day she said in front of a group of people whom she had invited for her birthday dinner that she would not pay for a meal for me, as I would sick it up anyway. I was furious. I would have liked to kick or punch her or shout at her. Instead, I said nothing and just gave her a nervous little smile."

LEARNING TO STAND YOUR GROUND

We can communicate our wants/needs/feelings in three different ways:

1. *Passive*
   Where your own wants/needs/feelings are silenced. This kind of communication may be given with a slumped body, downcast eyes, and a hesitant, giggly, or whining voice. It uses: "maybe", "I wonder if you could, only, just", "It's all right, don't bother".
2. *Assertive*
   Where you express your own wants, needs, and feelings, but also take into account the feelings of the person to whom you are talking.
3. *Aggressive*
   Where you only consider your own wants, needs, and feelings. Inappropriate anger or hostility is loudly or explosively uttered. There is use of threats: "you'd better", or put-downs: "come on, you must be kidding", or evaluative comments: "should", "I thought you would know better".

We all deal with different situations in these three ways. Women with eating difficulties often swing between the passive and aggressive poles and find it difficult to get onto a middle ground.

Think of the last time you behaved passively, suppressing your own feelings. Reconstruct the behaviour chain of this event (see chapter 2).

A. *Where, What, With Whom, and When?*
- What were your thoughts?
- What were the feelings (that you chose to suppress)?
- The thoughts that commonly lead to this pattern are:
  - "If I say something he/she won't like me"
  - "It's silly for me to be upset"
B. *Passive Behaviour*
- How, in what way, did you let someone walk over you?
C. *What Were the Positive and Negative Consequences of this?*

Assertive rather than passive behaviour is a skill you will need to learn and use as a way of finding the middle ground.

ANYTHING FOR A QUIET LIFE?

"Why should I learn to be assertive? Isn't it terribly risky?" you may ask. Whatever your reasons for not voicing your own needs, wants, and feelings, whilst in the short term it may seem easiest, in the long term it can seriously damage your physical and mental health.

- Not being assertive leads to a gradual build-up of frustration, which will keep your bulimia going and can also lead to other health problems like headaches and backaches.
- Others may sympathise with the poor downtrodden you and may seem to "like" your non-assertiveness. However, they'll soon become irritated by you, especially if you moan about how unfair life is or look so unwell with your bulimia and yet don't do anything about it.
- Ignoring conflict might make it go away in the short term, but in the long term tension and frustration increase. It is far healthier to deal with situations as they arise.

You may still say, "This all sounds like a lot of effort to me, and it carries the risk of alienating people around me. I am too frightened even to try." Nobody is saying you should change overnight to being assertive at all times in all situations, but you should at least have the choice as to whether or not you want to behave assertively in specific circumstances.

GROUND-RULES FOR ASSERTIVE BEHAVIOUR

Like everyone else, you have basic human rights: the right to hold and express your own opinions; the right to make mistakes; the right to refuse requests without guilt; the right to change your mind; the right to set your own priorities and goals; and the right to judge your own behaviour, thoughts, and emotions and to take responsibility for the consequences.

- Think ahead—before negotiating, be absolutely clear what you want to achieve and what your rights (and those of other people) are. Anticipate any possible objections, and work out your responses—being prepared will boost your confidence.
- Choose your timing if you can. Asking your boss for a pay rise as she pushes past your desk on the way to a meeting is not the right way to tackle it! Make an appointment with her to discuss the matter privately.
- When you make a request, be specific and direct. Avoid unassertive words like "only", "rather", and "maybe". Don't say, "I wondered whether maybe I could be put forward for promotion." Say, "Could I be put forward for promotion?"
- Criticise behaviour, not the person. Stick to facts and not judgements. Avoid words like "always", "never", and "impossible". Say something positive about the person or situation. After you have said what you had to say, don't hover. Don't undo what you said by apologising.
- When you have to say no, suggest alternatives. "I am afraid I can't help do the baby-sitting for you tonight, but I am free tomorrow if that's any help."
- Use the "broken record" technique on people who try to change the subject or convince you to reverse a decision. Repeat your point calmly, no matter what the other person says.
- Make eye contact. Adopt an upright and relaxed posture—shoulders down and arms by your side, not crossed defensively.

There are other techniques if you are being baited by criticism.

- Calmly accept that there may be some truth in what your critic says, but remain your own judge of what you do.
- Negative assertion: accept your errors or faults without having to apologise.
- Prompt criticism in order to use the information if it is helpful or to exhaust it if it is manipulative.

HOW TO PUT ASSERTIVENESS INTO PRACTICE

You will probably have seen some of the things outlined above in other books or in women's magazines, but you may still be wondering how to put it all into practice.

For situations where you can plan beforehand:

- Practice what you want to say in front of the mirror.
- Make a tape-recording of what you want to say.
- Role-play the situation with a friend, change roles, take on the person to whom you make the request.

There are, of course, situations where you have to think on your feet. You may have got so used to saying "yes" to other people's requests that you only notice after you have said "yes" that you really didn't want to take on the extra commitment. Remember, you have a right to change your mind. Ring up the person to whom you said "yes" and say, "I am sorry, but I will not be able to do the extra job after all."

You may also find it difficult to come up with an assertive response when someone puts you on the spot. You don't have to. You can tell the person later how you felt about what they said. Say, "I want to talk to you about what you said yesterday. It really hurt me when you said ..."

The first time you assert yourself will be terrifying, but you will improve with practice. You will find that behaving assertively leads to increased self-confidence, and that, in turn, will lead to more assertive behaviour. Gradually your life will become more balanced.

Below we give an example of a tricky situation one of our patients struggled with.

Ursula

Ursula is a well-liked, gentle sort of person, who in her spare time plays in an orchestra. One of the other players, a girl called Lynne, desperately tried to befriend Ursula. Lynne would ring Ursula up daily to tell her for hours about all the problems in her life, but she never seemed keen to listen to Ursula. She would repeatedly ask Ursula to go out with her in a way that was difficult to refuse: "You are not doing anything tonight. That's great. I have got two theatre tickets, would you like to go with me, I will pick you up in the car." Ursula felt overwhelmed at first but then got intensely irritated with Lynne. She avoided her as much as possible. She instructed her parents to tell Lynne she wasn't in when she rang. She thought of not going to the orchestra any more, although she enjoyed it very much. Part of her also felt sorry for Lynne, who seemed to have few other friends. She thought if she refused any of Lynne's approaches, she would hurt her and felt that, by accepting theatre tickets and other small favours, she had lost her right to assert herself and set limits in the relationship. It was obvious that something needed to be done. It was probable that, through partially avoiding Lynne, Ursula fuelled her persistence and that the only way to make herself freer again was to stand up to Lynne. This is how Ursula eventually asserted herself, by using the "broken record" technique:

Telephone Conversation

Ursula: "Hello, Ursula here."

Lynne (slightly reproachfully): "Hi, I've been trying to get hold of you all day, where have you been?"

Ursula (somewhat defensively): "Well, I had to go out and do a few things."

Lynne: "Are you in tonight?"

Ursula: "Yes, I am."

Lynne: "Are you doing anything specific?"

Ursula: "No nothing really, just watching TV."

Lynne (sounding enthusiastic): "Oh good, I thought I might just come over and see you. I'll pick up a pizza on the way. Would 8.00 p.m. be okay?"

Ursula: "Actually, I don't think I feel up to seeing anybody tonight. I just need some time to myself."

Lynne (somewhat surprised): "Oh, don't be such a bore. All that sitting around on your own does you no good whatsoever.

Ursula: "I am sorry you feel I am a bore, but I really don't feel up to seeing you tonight. Perhaps we could meet at the week-end."

Lynne (seductively): "I just thought it would be nice to meet tonight; there are a few new developments with Alan that I want to tell you about."

Ursula: "I'd love to hear about it, but I am just really not up to it tonight."

Lynne (more and more upset): "I don't understand what's going on. You are telling me you are doing nothing, and yet I can't come round. I think that's really selfish of you. You don't do that to an old friend."

Ursula: "I am sorry, but I really want to be on my own tonight."

It was obvious that as the telephone conversation progressed, Lynne was trying to make Ursula feel very uncomfortable and guilty. Ursula coped well by not rising to the bait and by not getting into an argument about whether or not she was acting selfishly.

FURTHER READING

Butler, P.E. (1982). *Self-assertion for women.* New York: Harper and Row.

Dickson. A. (1985). *A Woman in your own right. Assertiveness and you.* London: Quartet Books.

Hare, B. (1988). *Be assertive.* London: Macdonald Optima

CHAPTER TWELVE

The Seduction of Self-destruction

Alcohol and drug abuse, shoplifting and overspending are common in people with eating disorders. Underlying these problems are many different emotional reasons that parallel those covered in chapter 10 as underlying your binge eating. At times these patterns of behaviour are used as an escape route from the unpleasant effects of the eating disorder, numbing the feelings of guilt over bingeing or counteracting pangs of hunger. Or they may constitute a remedy to some other problem—for example, an inability to sleep or to relax is treated with alcohol or drugs. Alternatively, they are used in an attempt to "cure" some unpleasant state of mind, like boredom, depression, or anxiety. From rather innocent casual beginnings, enduring self-destructive patterns can emerge, as you will see from the cases described in this chapter.

THE SLIPPERY SLOPE OF BOOZE AND DRUGS

Strong social anxieties commonly lead to drinking/taking drugs. Especially if you "feel fat", you may find it difficult to go out unless you have drunk something.

Bridget
"I have always been a very shy person. Especially when I fancy someone, I get totally tongue-tied and clam up. I start pouring with sweat, and I can't think of anything to say. Other people must think I am totally boring when I am like that. My bulimia has made it

even more difficult to be relaxed with other people. The only way I can go out and have a good time is if I had something to drink. I usually have half a bottle of wine before I go out. Then I'll carry on drinking all night. I often can't really remember very much the next day, but others have told me that I behave totally outrageously when I am like that."

Of course, if you are always drunk or drugged when out, others will notice and will come to see you in an unfavourable light, which is what happened to Bridget.

"Some good friends have said to me that when I am drunk I am not very pleasant to be with. I stagger about, I make jokes that only I find funny, and I am very provocative with men. On one or two occasions I have actually got into bed with people whom I had never met and whom I would never want to see again when I am sober."

Sometimes drink/drugs are the result of the "I can't stand it, life is too awful" syndrome. Drink is used to ease the pain of living, as the examples of Julie and Moira show. But, of course, once a pattern has been established where your whole life revolves around drink/drugs, life is likely to remain awful and get worse.

Julie

Julie had been a promising dancer, but she had been thrown out of dance school because of her bulimia. "All my hopes were crushed. I hadn't learnt a thing. Frankly, I didn't want to do anything else. I had spent years dancing, thinking about being a dancer. I was so angry—angry with the school for throwing me out, angry with myself that I hadn't hidden my bulimia better from them, angry with my parents, with the whole world. Then I met Kevin, and we started a relationship. Kevin likes his drink, and soon we were out in the pub night after night. Neither of us had a job. My mum didn't like him, but I didn't care. I just drank and drank and drank, night after night. I couldn't stop. At some stage I tried to leave Kevin. He wouldn't let me. He got very angry and beat me up."

Moira

"I smoke dope every day. What am I like without it? Tense, anxious, eating myself up with worry about trivial things. I am the sort of person who will always find something to be worried about. I go over things endlessly in my mind—how I behaved in certain situations, what I should and shouldn't have said in certain conversations. Dope just blocks all of that out. Sometimes I worry about it, it really saps your energy levels, I have no drive, no motivation."

Some drugs, like amphetamines, help one lose weight, but the price to be paid is high: "When I was on amphetamines, I was so hyped up I could never sleep. My personality changed, and I became very suspicious." Many drugs available from private slimming clinics are of this type. These drugs are not prescribed in the NHS as it is realised that their side-effects far outweigh any value that they have.

Ecstasy

There has been a lot of publicity about Ecstasy, and this drug has been promoted as a designer drug with no untoward consequences. This is by no means true. A recent article by Henry, Jeffreys, and Dawling in the *Lancet* (1992, Vol. 340, pp. 384–387) reviews all the medical consequences, which range from liver failure to sudden death.

Caffeine and Artificial Sweeteners

Stop! Don't skip over this bit just because you are not taking any street drugs. What about your smoking? What about your caffeine and artificial sweetener consumption? We often forget what a powerful "drug" caffeine is. It can lead to anxiety, panic, and tremors. In excess, your sleep and thoughts get disturbed. It may become difficult to put your thoughts together; you may get suspicious of others. You should ask yourself the same questions as those outlined in the section on alcohol below, replacing the word "alcohol" with the particular "drug" you take. Again, if you answer more than three questions with "yes', you are probably heading towards being dependent on the drugs you are taking.

SHOULD I BE WORRIED ABOUT MY ALCOHOL INTAKE?

If you have an eating disorder, you run a much greater risk of becoming addicted to alcohol and drugs, for a number of reasons. Research has consistently found that problems with alcohol and drugs are much more common amongst families of women with eating disorders. We do not know exactly what causes the same type of problem to run through the generations. What is passed on may be some genetic vulnerability, or it may be that if drinking a lot is a way of responding to problems in your family, you grow up picking up the same way of behaving. There are also important physical reasons—your restriction of food—which make you vulnerable to the seductive powers of alcohol. Your body will quickly learn that this is the only source of calories you will allow yourself. This exaggerates the craving for alcohol.

Alcoholic drinks have "empty" calories; they contain none of the additional substances such as minerals and vitamins that are required for health. Moreover, the body's methods of detoxifying alcohol use up the vitamin reserves of the body. You therefore run an increased risk of vitamin deficiency if you drink alcohol. These deficiencies lead to brain damage—your memory is particularly at risk.

What Are the Safe Limits?

To calculate your weekly intake, it is best to count up the units you drink:

1 unit of alcohol = half a pint of beer
= a single measure of spirits
= a glass of wine
= a small glass of sherry
= a measure of vermouth or aperitif

Drinks poured at home are usually much more generous than pub or restaurant measures. So, in calculating your units, you need to take this into account. Write down your daily intake in your diary for a week.

You may have read that for women up to 14 units a week, spread throughout the week, carries no long-term health risks (for men up to 21 units). However, for the reasons described above, we cannot be sure what level is safe for women with eating disorders with their precarious state of nutrient balance. If you concentrate your drinking into, say, two bouts and get drunk, you're increasing the risks to yourself even without an eating disorder. If you drink more than 22 units per week (for men more than 36), damage to your health is likely. Your liver and stomach can both be affected. Your concentration may be poor, and all sorts of personal and social problems may be building up. There may be financial and legal problems, problems at work and home, and sexual difficulties, too.

Answer the following questions as honestly as possible[1]:

- Do you often drink too much? Do you often think you should cut down?
- Does alcohol cause problems for you and make you feel guilty?
- Has anyone ever objected to your drinking or criticised you about it?
- Have you ever had a drink in the morning to steady your nerves or to get rid of a hangover?

If the answer to one or several of these questions is YES, go on.

- Do you often find that, when you start drinking, you end up drinking more than you were planning to?
- Do you often try to cut down or stop drinking alcohol?
- Do you spend a lot of time drinking, being high, or being hung over?

- Do you ever drink while doing something where it might be dangerous to drink at all (like driving)?
- Do you drink so often that you start to drink instead of working or spending time at hobbies or with your family or friends?
- Does your drinking cause problems with other people?
- Does your drinking cause you significant psychological or physical problems?
- Do you find you need to drink a lot more in order to get high than you did when you first started to drink?
- Do you ever have the shakes when you cut down drinking?

If you answered more than three questions with a definite YES, you are heading towards being dependent on alcohol. As long as you are on alcohol, it will be extremely difficult to make progress with your eating disorder. You may want to contact Alcohol Concern to see what services are available (the address is given at the end of the book).

Have the Guts to Stop or Cut Down Your Alcohol Consumption

If you decided from what you read above that you have problems with alcohol, you should cut down drinking or even avoid alcohol altogether. Not drinking is something that is becoming much more socially acceptable. Think of the parallel case of smoking. Five or ten years ago, people who objected to others smoking in their presence were seen as weird, silly, or wet, and if they complained, they had to endure sarcastic comments and abuse. Nowadays, with increased knowledge about the health risks of active and passive smoking, it is the smokers who are at the receiving end of the criticism. This point was reached by public campaigns, but also because many people in their private lives stood up to the tyrannical behaviour of smokers.

Can you show some personal bravery if others bully you into drinking? "Oh come on, don't be a spoil-sport, why don't you just have a tiny drink?" It can be very difficult to resist someone who is determined to get you to drink. But if your friends only accept you if you drink with them, and in large amounts, are they really worth your while?

How to Cut Down

- Take small sips only. Count the number of sips it takes to finish a glass, and then try increasing the number for the next glass, and so on.
- Do something else enjoyable while drinking that will help distract attention from the glass—for example, listening to music, talking, doing a cross-word puzzle, and so on.

- Instead of drinking your customary, favourite type of drink, change to something new. Changing the type of drink can help break old habits and reduce the amount drunk.
- Drink more slowly, and concentrate on the flavour.
- Copy a slow drinker. Identify someone who drinks slowly and shadow them, not picking up the glass until they do.
- Put the glass down after each sip. If you hold the glass, you will drink more often. Do something else with your hand instead of lifting the glass to the lips.
- Top up spirits with non-alcoholic drinks.
- As much as you can, buy your own drinks. If you have to go along with sharing rounds, do not buy yourself a drink when it is your round, or order a non-alcoholic drink.
- Take days of rest, when you don't drink alcohol, at least one day per week, or preferably two, three, or even four days per week. Take up other forms of entertainment or relaxation.
- Start drinking later than usual. For example, go to the pub later.
- Learn to refuse drinks. Role-play ways of saying no to drinks. Perhaps this is the most important assertiveness skill you need to learn. Say, for example, "No thanks, I'm cutting down", or "I am not drinking tonight, I've got a bad stomach".

Remember also, alcohol removes inhibition and therefore increases the likelihood of binges.

DO YOU LIKE RUSSIAN ROULETTE?

Although the risk of being shot whilst shoplifting is low, the sobering fact is that most people get caught at some point. So why do so many bright and otherwise law-abiding people with eating disorders take what is a considerable risk of public humiliation, court appearance, a criminal record, and, in some cases, even being sent to prison?

There is a multitude of reasons: Some steal food when they have a strong urge to binge, or have run out of money to buy binge food. Others take things, like items of clothing or other items, that they don't need or like. Often they can't explain why they do it. The exact cause for this seemingly irrational behaviour is not understood. It has been thought that being starved has something to do with it. For example, it is known that animals who are starved hoard things. In a famous starvation experiment carried out in the 1950s in the United States, the men who participated (who were deliberately starved) began to collect and hoard all sorts of objects.

Repeated shoplifting can also be a way of dealing with boredom and depression by creating a thrill. This sense of excitement can be addictive and can lead to more and more risktaking.

Louise

"I have shop-lifted regularly over the last five years. It's got a lot worse since my bulimia started. As a child I was very unhappy, and I sometimes stole sweets. Now it's mainly make-up or earrings. I tend to do it when I am in one of my bingeing phases. I don't tend to do it when I am dieting and feel in control. It gives me a kick, it's exciting and terrifying."

Over time, you may get more and more hooked on it and convinced that you are not going to be caught, but, of course, most people do eventually get caught.

Claire

Claire began to steal things from shops a few years after her bulimia had begun. She would take clothes, food, cosmetics, and magazines. She kept long and detailed lists of everything she had stolen. "I still don't know why I did it. I just had to do it. It was like an obsession. It made me feel I was in control. I knew I was taking lots of risks, I even went into shops where they had automatic cameras installed. Maybe subconsciously I was waiting to be caught." Claire did get caught after a couple of years of regular stealing. She made no attempt to hide what she had done; the police found the lists of items she had stolen, and she had to serve a prison sentence of several months. "Prison wasn't the worst thing. What was much worse was that the whole thing was published in the local press, with my name and address. Until then I hadn't told anyone about my bulimia, and to have that dragged out was the most awful thing."

IF I WERE A RICH MAN ...

Overspending is another self-destructive way of dealing with depression, emptiness, and boredom. Although it doesn't usually get people into legal trouble, it causes problems of its own. Many bulimic women get into such hopeless financial situations with their compulsive spending that they owe thousands of pounds to various creditors. Once you see no chance of paying your debts off, you may think you might as well carry on and, thereby, get deeper and deeper into trouble.

Sharon

Sharon is a single mother on social security: "I have been feeling very fed up and down lately, nothing gives me pleasure, nothing interests me. Then I suddenly got this catalogue in and began to order various things, including a hoover, a mixer, some other bits and pieces for the kitchen. For a little while it made me feel better, like I had achieved something. That didn't last very long, though. Altogether it came up to £500. When it arrived, I didn't even open the boxes to check the contents. The stuff's been sitting in my cupboard for three weeks now, completely untouched.

Often the trap of overspending stops a person from getting on with what they'd like to do, like going on holidays, moving house, doing a college course, and so on.

Lisa

Lisa, a typist, lives with her parents. She owes the bank £2,000 and another £1,500 to her parents. "I can't really afford to buy anything at the moment. It'll be ages before I have paid everything off. I'd love to move out of home but I can't. There is no way I could afford to pay rent, given my current financial situation. Most of my money goes on clothes—clothes that I often don't wear, not even once. It's as if I am desperately trying to find the right thing."

Do You Overspend or Steal?

- What is your pattern?
- Note down in your diary (Chapter 2—the ABC technique) the circumstances of overspending/stealing.
  - How do you feel at the time?
  - How do you feel afterwards?
  - What would happen if you stopped?
  - Is it that you don't allow yourself any other rewards, pleasures, or excitement?
  - Can you find other exciting or simply nice things to do?
- If your problem is shop-lifting, some people find it helpful to imagine the worst thing they can possibly think of in order to prevent themselves from doing something like stealing. In Claire's case, a nightmare scenario really did come true. Write down your own personal nightmare scenario, and try to imagine it every time you have the urge to steal something.
- If your problem is overspending, you must make a start with paying off your debts, no matter how slowly you go. It does not help to hide all the demands for payment at the back of the drawer, even though this is a common way women with eating disorders try to cope. A bank manager is used to dealing with this problem and will be able to come up with practical solutions. Is there any friend or family member in whom you can confide about this problem? Can you get them to help you by looking after your cheque book or credit cards? Can they help you budget?

NOTE

1. Adapted from Spitzer, R.L., Williams, J.B.W., Gibbon, M., & First, M.B. (1989). *Structured Clinical Interview for DSM-III-R: Non-patient Edition.* (SCIO, 9/1/89 Revision). New York: New York State Psychiatric Institute, Biometrics Research Department.

FURTHER READING

Curran, V., & Golombok, S. (1985). *Bottling it up.* London: Faber and Faber.

Chick, J., & Chick, J. (1984). *Drinking problems: Information and advice for the individual, family and friends.* Edinburgh: Churchill Livingstone.

Miller, W.R., & Munoz, R.F. (1983). *How to control your drinking.* London: Sheldon Press.

Tyrer, P. (1986). *How to stop taking tranquillisers.* London: Sheldon Press.

CHAPTER THIRTEEN

The Web of Life: Parents, Partners, Children, and Friends

HOME, SWEET HOME

Especially if you are still living at home, your eating disorder may cause a lot of upset in your family. Your parents may get angry with you for raiding the cupboards or for rejecting their meals. They may feel guilty and blame themselves for your eating disorder. They may alternate between trying to help by cooking for you and buying you special diet foods and angrily telling you to "snap out" of your "silly" eating problem.

You may feel that they don't understand you, that they treat you like a child, that they are getting at you, or you may be upset about the upset you cause them. It is difficult living with other people when you suffer from an eating disorder, but it is equally difficult living with someone who has an eating disorder.

Elizabeth

Elizabeth had had bulimia nervosa for several years. Her parents knew about this, especially her mother, who had read any book on the topic of eating disorders that she could lay her hands on. After a period of living away from home, Elizabeth moved back home because of financial difficulties. "My mother was observing me incredibly carefully. Yet she would never mention my eating disorder. She was just treating me with kid gloves. I found out from my boyfriend that she had talked to him behind my back, telling him that if he had any problem with me he could always come to her. When he told me this, I was very cross. Am I some sort of invalid? Too fragile to be talked to? I think that my mother is quite ashamed about my problem, that's why she can't talk about it directly."

How to Improve Your Relationship with Your Parents

- If you haven't told your parents about your eating problem, think hard about whether you should. What are the gains and losses? Often parents have an inkling that something is wrong with your eating anyway, and to tell them can be a huge relief to them and to you.
- If you have told them about your eating problem and somehow this has not made matters better, they may need more information about eating disorders to be able to understand and help you. Could you give your parents this book to read? Could you suggest to them to attend a Parents' Group of the Eating Disorder Association (see address at the end of the book)?
- Spell out to your parents how they can help you. Be specific and direct. Positive suggestions work better than negative ones. So don't say, "You don't understand me, you are getting it all wrong." Say, "It would help me if I could eat with you in the evenings. Eating one meal a day with other people would be a huge step forward for me."
- Remember, your parents are only human; they are bound to get it wrong at times, just like you are. Don't expect them only to ask you about your eating problem when you feel you want to be asked. They can't read your mind.
- If things are very bad, maybe you should consider moving out. What you shouldn't do is feel upset about living at home and not do anything about it.

Briony

Briony, an 18-year-old student, was the youngest of a family of four. Her father was a vicar. She had been the favourite of her parents as she did very well at school and was a gifted piano player. When she developed anorexia nervosa at the age of 16 and nearly died, her parents felt awful—as if they, personally, were to blame. However, they found it even more impossible to understand or tolerate Briony's bulimic symptoms, which she developed after her anorexia. Her raiding the larder at night was seen by her family as a sign of greed and moral wickedness. "My mother and I had a shouting match every day. We had always been a very quiet, harmonious family, where people tried to talk to sort out problems."

Briony realised that her eating problem was destroying her relationship with her parents. She moved into a small flat of her own. "Once I was there, the communication between me and my parents began gradually to get better. My father actually helped me to decorate my flat. My mother agreed to go shopping with me once a week, as I had lost any idea of how much I would need. Gradually our wounds are beginning to heal. I go to see my parents every Sunday. I still feel very sad when I return to my empty flat on Sunday night, yet I think there would not have been any other solution for us."

Write a balance sheet on the pros and cons of living at home.

- If, on balance, you feel you should move out, think through carefully what the alternatives could be. Living totally alone in a bedsit in an area where you don't know anybody can make matters worse. Could you find a friend to share?

FRIENDS

Sheila MacLeod, in her book *The Art of Starvation*, said, "the anorexic has a fundamental mistrust of personal relationships which have so often proved to be symbolic and destructive .... on the other hand she has a longing for a good relationship with another person who will understand and accept her for what she feels herself to be." Your eating disorder may make it very difficult for you to trust anybody, especially if you have been let down before. You may find it difficult to be a reliable and dependable friend yourself. You may drop out of arrangements you have made with friends because food is involved. You may drop out of going for meals or parties because you find it too frightening. Perhaps you see yourself as so apart from the rest of the world that you actually feel what is the point of meeting with friends who don't know what's bothering you? Having dropped out of things a few times, you may drop out because you don't want to face your friends' reactions. It is obvious that if your friends don't know about your eating disorder, they will get very fed up with you and find your behaviour difficult to understand.

One way to improve the situation might be to tell your friends about your eating problem.

With a Little Help from My Friends

Friends often are much easier to talk to than parents. Before you tell them, think about what their response might be:

- If your answer is, "they won't want to know, they won't like me if I tell them", you should ask yourself, is this really true? Or is it more likely to be a fear YOU have? If you are pretty certain your friends will not respond positively, maybe you should reconsider whether they are worth your while to be nurtured as friends.

- If the answer is, "they will be sympathetic, but they won't understand", maybe you need to educate them about your problem. You could give them this book, for instance.
- If your answer is, "of course my best friend would not think badly of me because of my eating problem, but still I couldn't tell her. ... " You should think why it is so difficult for you to confide. What do you have to lose? Getting better involves letting go of your problem a bit, letting others in to listen and support. If you need to keep your problem totally secret, perhaps that says something about your motivation to change. Perhaps it isn't quite as strong as you thought.

Perhaps you have told your friends about your eating disorder long ago but you still worry about the effect your eating disorder is having on your relationship with them. You should ask yourself the following:

- Do you make an effort to look after your friendships, or do you always wait for someone else to ring you? Making the first move in a relationship is very frightening. Maybe you feel, "I don't want to be seen to need somebody." Perhaps you fear people will only go out with you out of pity. Remember, we all depend on others. Needing others and admitting you want their company is not weakness, it is actually a strength. How do YOU feel when someone rings YOU up? Is your first thought that they are weak for wanting to be with you? Surely not!

Making Friends

Perhaps you have already lost some or all of your friends or have gradually grown away from them. If there aren't any old friendships you could rekindle, maybe you need to make a fresh start. Here are a few suggestions that may help you in making the first steps towards meeting new people.

- It is important not to set your sights too high. You will not make very deep friendships within the space of a few weeks. However, you may be able to have regular social contact with people who you feel are quite nice. And that is definitely better than festering alone at home.
- Don't be too choosy. Go out with people, even if you don't think they are going to become your best friend. Firstly, your initial instincts may be proved wrong. And secondly, these people may introduce you to their friends.
- Expect setbacks and rejections. You may find yourself in the position of having to ask a number of people to do something with you before

you get a positive response. This is very disheartening, and you may feel very tempted to think, "nobody likes me". Remember, there are many possible reasons why someone might not be able to go out with you. Most of these reasons will have nothing to do with you. Try to think of examples when you had to turn someone down because you were busy, tired, going out with someone else, having to take the dog to the vet's, or because you had an exam the next day. Most people actually like being asked out, even if they can't make it.

- If you join an evening class to meet people, expect that some classes will not generate much contact outside the actual class. Certain classes will make it much more likely that you get to know others. It is much easier to chat whilst you do pottery than during a maths course.

Below is a list of suggestions of how to meet people. Think of some ideas which you might add to the list.

- evening classes
- sports clubs
- environmental organisations
- pressure groups (Amnesty, Greenpeace)
- church activities
- invite your neighbours over for a drink
- invite work colleagues over

SEXUAL RELATIONSHIPS

Sexual relationships are a sore point for many people.

Perhaps you have watched your parents in very unhappy or unsuccessful relationships. Perhaps you were sexually abused during your childhood or had frightening or unpleasant sexual encounters as an adult. Maybe this has left you feeling suspicious and wary of sexual relationships, or it has made you feel you are not a worthwhile person, and you therefore continue to plunge yourself into sexual relationships that are unrewarding, destructive, and undermine your self-esteem further. Whatever your particular pattern is, you will need time to think about it and change it.

Are You Frightened of Sex?

The thought of having a physical relationship may be absolutely terrifying for you. Perhaps this is part of a general fear of getting too close to anyone, or you feel so bad about your body that you can't bear the thought of someone touching you—or maybe you have been brought up in a family where sex was regarded as a taboo, or perhaps you have been abused.

Kate

Kate was a 25-year-old teacher who had developed an eating disorder when she was 15. She had never had a boyfriend, which she was very sad about. "I just couldn't handle the thought of anyone getting close to me, but at the same time I felt desperately lonely." All her male friends were gay. She shared a house with one of them. He was her closest friend and helped her a great deal in overcoming her eating disorder. She practically spent all her spare time with him. When her eating disorder improved, she began to recognise that her friendship was safe and rewarding, but also rather limited, and that it stopped her from meeting other people. She was very frightened of moving out, but in the end she decided that this was her only chance to change her situation.

If you are frightened of sexual contact:

- Ask yourself whether, like Kate, you are hiding away without the opportunity to meet someone? If you want to overcome your fear, maybe you need to change your lifestyle.
- If your fear of sex is fear of the unknown, maybe you should take some steps to remedy the deficits in your education. A reading list is given at the end of the chapter.
- If you have a partner, think very hard whether you can let them know how you feel about sex?

The Wrong Man

Perhaps you repeatedly get into relationships with the wrong partner—someone who initially attracts and excites you, but then things turn sour repeatedly in the same way. Instead of turning from frog into prince, your partners stay frogs no matter how much you kiss them.

It may be that you are searching for someone who displays characteristics you would like to have but may also lack values and attributes you hold and cherish, and so it goes wrong.

Vanessa

Vanessa was a very image-conscious young woman, who spent all her money on designer clothes and make-up. "Men see me just as a sexy blonde." All her boyfriends were good-looking muscular types. "Whenever I go to the night club with one of my boyfriends, people will turn round and look at us admiringly. I rather enjoy that, and I think all the preparation beforehand was worth it." All her boyfriends were extremely jealous of other men and whilst initially in a relationship she enjoyed this, later on she would find

Kiss! Kiss!

Still a frog?

Nothing changes

it irritating and claustrophobic. One of her boyfriends beat her up out of jealousy, and another one created a fuss in a night-club and they were banned. "I have often asked myself, why do I always go for the same type of man? I still don't know why. I am just not attracted to someone who isn't good-looking no matter how nice they are."

If you repeatedly get involved with the wrong type of men, ask yourself:

• What is it that attracts you to that kind of man?
• What does your choice say about you?
• Are you drawn to people who display features that you are lacking?

Changing your pattern may be difficult. Remember, the first step towards change is recognising and accepting that there is a problem.

Promiscuity

To go through a phase of short-lived sexual relationships in a trial-and-error fashion is perhaps not that uncommon for many young people. However, this pattern can become a problem.

Deirdre

Deirdre is a 26-year-old nurse. She has never had a steady boyfriend. Since her teens she has had many brief relationships, none of them lasting for longer than a few weeks. She has also had quite a few one-night stands. "I find it very easy to start relationships, and initially I am very keen on whoever I am with. But that seems to change quite quickly, and I get very bored, and I then have to get rid of them very quickly. A few times I have had a one-night stand when I have drunk too much, and that's at times been quite unpleasant."

Yvonne

Yvonne is 30. Her father, whom she has never met, was from Jamaica; her mother, who was Scottish, was an alcoholic. Yvonne grew up in a children's home, where she was bullied. When she was 12 she was raped by some older boys. She was too scared to tell anyone. She became a prostitute when she was 17. She is now unemployed and lives on her own with her two children. She has never used contraception. She has been pregnant 12 times altogether. She had 5 miscarriages and 5 abortions.

If you are changing your partners more quickly than Casanova, ask yourself why you are doing it:

- Do you get a kick out it? Does it feel like something slightly forbidden, slightly dangerous? If that's the case, what other sources of excitement do you have in your life?
- Sometimes promiscuity is the result of extremely low self-esteem. Do you plunge yourself into relationships because you feel you somehow don't deserve any better? Or to make yourself feel better? In the long run this is going to make you feel worse about yourself.
- Are you usually drunk when you get sexually involved? Why do you let yourself?
- Do you use sex as a way of pleasing others? Is it the only way you know of gaining acceptance (love)?

Whatever your reasons for promiscuity are:

- Make sure you protect yourself against pregnancy and sexually transmitted disease.

CHILDREN

Periods usually stop in anorexia nervosa as a direct result of starvation. Many women with eating disorders worry therefore, about whether they will be able to have babies, what a pregnancy would be like for them, and whether they might damage their unborn baby. We have tried to answer some of the most commonly asked questions in this area.

Will I Be Able to Get Pregnant?

Very little is known about the fertility of women with anorexia nervosa after they have gained weight. What is known, though, is that some women get pregnant despite very irregular or even absent periods, even though their eating disorder is still active.

Could I Have Damaged My Baby?

- If, by the time you get pregnant, you have overcome your eating disorder and you are at a healthy weight and eating normally, there is nothing to be worried about.
- If you starve yourself regularly during pregnancy, your baby is at risk of being born prematurely and underweight. Both these factors will make the baby more susceptible to illness. We don't know what effects repeated vomiting or abuse of laxatives have on the unborn child.

What Will Happen to My Eating Disorder during Pregnancy?

Many women with eating disorders who get pregnant manage to get their symptoms under control during pregnancy because their wish not to harm their baby is very strong. After the baby is born, many go back to their old habits. So, if you are planning to get pregnant, it is definitely best to try to sort your eating disorder out first.

Rosie

Rosie used approximately 100 laxative tablets every time she binged. The after-effects of this were terrible for her—she suffered severe pain and massive diarrhoea. During a short-lived relationship with a man she got pregnant and decided to keep the baby. "As soon as I knew I was pregnant, I knew that I had to stop taking my laxatives. Once during pregnancy when I over-ate, I took some laxatives on the spur of the moment, without thinking about it. Afterwards I got so worried about having damaged my baby that for the rest of my pregnancy I didn't touch the stuff at all. Now I have got a beautiful baby boy of 6 months. He has transformed my life. I am still breast-feeding a little, so I am still not taking any laxatives, but I know that when he is not going to be dependent on me physically any more I might easily fall back."

Will I Cope with Putting on Weight during Pregnancy?

The prospect of weight gain during pregnancy can be daunting—whether or not you suffer from an eating disorder. Many women worry about whether they will be able to return to their previous shape after pregnancy. In our experience, eating-disordered mothers have similarly varied responses to the weight and shape changes of pregnancy as non-eating-disordered mothers. Some cope well, others feel huge.

I Am Worried about Being a Bad Mother

Many women with eating disorders are very good mothers. It must be said, however, that the stresses of handling an eating problem and raising a child sometimes do take their toll. Some bulimic mothers may find it very difficult to feed their children because they are stuck between the extreme poles of total control or no control.

Wendy

Wendy was a single mother of a 7-year-old daughter. Her bulimia had started before her child's birth. "I have never been able to eat with her, which I find incredibly sad. She only has me, and really we should eat together. But I simply find it too difficult. I serve her tea and then busy myself with something else. When she has finished, I quickly throw the leftovers away. She used to accept my behaviour unquestioningly, but now that she is older, of course she wants to know why I never sit down with her. The other day she told me how nice it had been when she visited a friend's house where the whole family had sat down together for their tea.

Another problem is, we are quite hard up, and I often say to her, you can't have this or that because we have no money. It makes me feel terrible to have to deny her things just because I waste so much money on my binges."

Others find it difficult to get the correct balance of discipline that every child needs.

Ellie

Ellie had a boy aged 9 and a girl aged 5. She had little support from her husband in bringing up the children as he was a long-distance lorry driver and often away from home for long stretches of time. "Both my children are quite difficult, especially Oliver, my 9-year-old, who is quite a handful. When I am in one of my bingeing phases, I have no time or energy to do anything with them other than the absolute basics. I let them watch the TV for hours whilst I am in the kitchen stuffing myself. During these phases I don't manage to be firm with them, and both of them tend to play up much more then. At other times, when I am not bingeing, I try to make up to them—I read with them, take them to the park, or invite some of their friends round to play. I also don't let them get away with it if they are naughty. But I somehow fear my inconsistent handling is going to damage them. In fact, Oliver's school said he was quite badly behaved, and we will have to go and see a child psychologist."

If you have children and are worried about the effect of your eating disorder on them, ask yourself the following questions:

• Are you right to be worried? What is the evidence for your worry? Are you trying to be "a good-enough mother" or are you trying to be a perfect mother? Is it possible that the thinking traps outlined in chapter 10 might trip you up in the area of mothering, too?

If, on close questioning, you decide that, well, basically you are doing fine, other people seem to think your children are delightful and they are thriving, you need read no further.

If you remain worried, what are you worried about? Their diet, their behaviour, their emotional development?

• Use the problem solving approach outlined in chapter 2 to define the problem and think of solutions.

If you are worried about your children's diet, bear in mind the following:

• Don't try to restrict their diet. Children are amazingly good at knowing how much they need.
• Don't ban sweets totally in an attempt to protect your children from an eating disorder. The more you create an aura of forbidden food, the more interested they will become in sweets.
• Try to persuade them to eat some fruit and vegetable every day, but don't panic if your child doesn't share your predilection for health foods.

If you find that you alone or you and your partner can't deal with the worries and difficulties you have with the children, go and get some advice. Don't be ashamed to do so! It can save yourself and your children a lot of misery. Do you have good friends with children? Can you talk to them about your worries? Or maybe your doctor can help or your health visitor.

FURTHER READING

Amodeo, J., & Wentworth, K. (1986). *A guide to successful relationships*. London: Arkana.

Beck, A.T. (1988). *Love is never enough. How couples can overcome conflicts and solve relationship problems through cognitive therapy*. London: Penguin Books.

Byrne, K. (1987). *The parent's guide to anorexia and bulimia*. New York: Schocken Books.

Comfort, A. (1982). *The joy of love*. London: Quartet Books.

Dickson, A. (1985). *The mirror within*. London: Quartet Books.

Friday, N. (1986). *My secret garden*. London: Quartet Books.

Norwood, R. (1986). *Women who love too much! When You keep wishing and hoping he'll change*. London: Arrow Books.

Skynner, R., & Cleese, J. (1983). *Families and how to survive them*. London: Methuen.

CHAPTER FOURTEEN

Working to Live, Living to Work

Having a regular day-time occupation, whether it is paid work, housework, studying, or voluntary work, is an important part of our lives. If it's the right job for the right person, work can be an important source of self-esteem. It can provide pleasure, challenge, and stimulation. Very few people actually feel that positively about their job at all times, but they still appreciate the fact that their work gives them independence, a sense of purpose, and a daily routine.

Many sufferers of eating disorders have difficulties with their work. Such problems can have very different sources. They may simply be the result of difficult work conditions like a nasty boss, long working hours, shiftwork, low pay, or sexual harassment. Sometimes sufferers of bulimia—because they feel bad about themselves or because they are frightened of change—get into, and stay in, bad jobs. Problems at work can also arise as a result of a mismatch between the job and the person doing it.

SOME COMMON WORK PROBLEMS

I Don't Have a Job

Whilst there are many reasons for being out of work, some people lose their job as a result of their eating disorder.

Hazel

Hazel was 19. She had wanted to be a nurse all her life. She was overjoyed when she got into a nursing course at a major teaching hospital. However, she dropped out of it within a few weeks "as it didn't seem like what I had imagined it at all". Her parents were very critical of her decision and felt she should not have given up so quickly. In order to earn some money, she began to work in a restaurant. "I had to give that up, too, as I just couldn't cope with all the food around. The owner began to notice that bits were missing." She then took up a job in a trendy boutique as a shop assistant. "Everybody there was very slim and figure-conscious. I found that very difficult, especially if I had a binge the night before. I just couldn't face going in feeling all fat and horrible. So in the end I lost the job." She spent two months at home with her eating disorder getting worse, and with constant criticisms from her mother. Although she'd routinely go to the job centre, she never actually went to any job interviews. "I had totally lost my confidence."

If you are out of a job and frightened of starting again, you should think about the following:

- Being out of work is bound to make your eating disorder worse due to lack of structure and boredom.
- Perhaps your eating disorder is so severe that you feel you can't hold down a full-time job. You may be right. Maybe you should think of doing a part-time job or voluntary work, just to get you going and to build up your confidence.
- Perhaps you are telling yourself that you are just waiting for the right job to come along. Whilst there is certainly something to be said for trying to find the right job, you should try to be honest with yourself and ask yourself whether the right job is likely to come along. Maybe you are just avoiding making a start.
- If you are frightened of going to job interviews, is there anyone who could help you with this problem? It may be very useful to role-play such a situation. If there isn't anyone who you trust enough to do this with you, write down a list of things you may be asked in a job interview. Think in particular about how you are going to explain periods of being out of work. Prepare an answer to each question, and rehearse them aloud to yourself. Do this a few times so you sound fluent and convincing. The better you prepare yourself, the more likely you are going to be successful.

I Am Not in the Right Job

A lot of misery is caused if you perpetually push yourself to do things you are not cut out to do. Many sufferers of eating disorders have punishingly high expectations of what they should achieve in their jobs. These high expectations may be the result of high expectations your parents had, or still have, of you, and in an attempt to please them you may have gone along with them. Or there may be an attempt to compete with a brother or sister who has done well.

Virginia

Virginia came from a family with very high academic expectations. Her father was a university professor. He and her two older brothers had degrees from Cambridge, and it was expected that she would follow in their footsteps. "It was unthinkable in my family not to go to university." At school Virginia had never been very interested in the academic subjects, and she was very unsure what she wanted to do. "The thought of going to university and spending more time studying horrified me. I wanted to get straight into work and earn some money. I knew I was not cut out to be an academic high-flyer like my brothers. Everybody in my family told me I'd regret it if I didn't make the most of my education." With a great deal of hard work and a lot of pressure from her parents, Virginia eventually got into university and started a law course. "My parents were so proud of me, it was unbelievable. On the surface I was pleased, as everybody in my family told me I was doing the right thing. Underneath it all, I was panic-stricken. I just knew I wasn't cut out to be a lawyer. I thought it was utterly boring." Not surprisingly, Virginia's eating disorder, which had started whilst she was still at school in the run-up to her A-levels, got much worse at university. In the end she dropped out of her course. She then took up a job in a big department store as a trainee buyer. She enjoyed this work and was very good at it. "I am still very cross with my parents for pushing me so hard. I know they only meant well, but they got it all wrong."

On the other hand, holding yourself back and aiming too low will cause you to be resentful, unfulfilled, and bored.

Kimberley

Kimberley had worked as a VDU operator in a bank for many years. She was hard-working and reliable. She always got positive feedback from her supervisor in her annual review. Many other people, who had started after her, went for promotion and got it, but she was too frightened to apply as she was worried about making a mess of the interview. She also felt that, due to her bulimia, she might not be able cope with more responsibility. At the same time she resented being overtaken by younger colleagues who didn't have half as much experience as she had. "When I thought about the situation rationally, I knew I could do a better job than they did. The longer the whole situation dragged on, the more resentful I felt about the whole situation."

- Write out for yourself how Kimberley should organise herself to plan for promotion. Use chapter 2 for help.

Juliette

Juliette was a bright young woman who had an English degree. As a child she had been her father's favourite, and he had always emphasised the importance of a good career to her. She felt that he was quite disappointed when she studied English instead of law, as he had done. After university, she had a couple of jobs with publishing firms, but she couldn't cope with them due to her eating disorder. She then worked on and off as a temporary secretary. She was very unhappy with this, as she felt the work was boring. She had a vague idea of wanting to work in the media but was too scared to make a go of it. "I felt that if I did try it and I failed, I'd be worse off than ever. I also knew that everybody in my family would be extremely sceptical if I tried yet another new career and that I would be unable to cope with that. I often looked at job adverts and considered applying, but then I'd get too panic-stricken. I felt trapped by my indecision." Juliette came into therapy for her eating disorder. She began to realise that she might easily go on wasting much more time being a temp and that it was unrealistic that she'd be given a dream job in the media in view of her work record. She decided to apply for a permanent secretarial post within a television company, as this would allow her to take a good look at a field of work in which she was interested and help her decide whether she really wanted to get deeper into it.

- Imagine you were Juliette using problem solving techniques (chapter 2) to draw up a decision making sheet.

Workaholics

Some people spend practically all their waking hours working. Very few of them actually enjoy this. If you are one of those few, you need read no further. Most workaholics, however, overwork out of a sense of battling against personal failure or out of perfectionism ("If I don't give my everything ... I might as well not bother ... people will think I am no good.") Re-read chapter 10 and try to work out where your striving for success and perfectionism comes from. Overwork takes it's toll by making an eating disorder worse.

Sylvia

Sylvia was a trainee accountant. She worked in a firm where it was simply expected that employees worked for 10 to 12 hours a day. Often she'd have to go in at week-ends to be able to meet deadlines. She was also working for her accountancy exams. She never had any breaks at work. When she finally came home in the evening, she needed several glasses of whisky to wind down, and then she'd have a binge. She often felt that she couldn't go on like this for much longer. She found it very difficult to come for treatment, as it interfered with her punishing schedule. It took Sylvia a long time to realise that she had a part to play in creating some of the pressures at work for herself. It turned out that she worked harder than any of her colleagues. As she never had any breaks, she was often overtired and therefore inefficient and slow. Sylvia was asked to allow herself to have three breaks in the day and to eat something each time she had a break. "It was very difficult for me to do this. I had to tell myself over and over again that I wouldn't get better without it. There were always temptations to get out of having a break." Once Sylvia had got into a routine of having breaks, she managed to work much more efficiently and actually began to enjoy her job again. Her evening binges gradually lessened.

Sometimes overworking can be the result of an exaggerated sense of duty or responsibility.

Eleni

Eleni was the oldest daughter of a Greek Cypriot family. For many years her parents had worked extremely hard to build up a small restaurant. "They always said they did it so that my sisters and me would have it better than them one day." Eleni worked as a nurse and lived at home. She felt to show her gratitude she ought to help her parents, so all her spare time and at week-ends she waitressed in her parents' restaurant. When she occasionally had an evening to herself she was much too tired to go out and instead binged. Her younger sisters helped out much less. The middle sister was a student and claimed she was far too busy to help, and the youngest one had left home and was living with an English boyfriend. "My sisters are really rather selfish. My parents complain about them to me, but at the end of the day they do let them get away with it, and all the helping falls back on me." Eleni felt that she couldn't go her own way, as this would be like betraying her parents.

If you habitually overwork, you have a problem with balancing your "shoulds" and "wants". Go to chapter 8 and re-read the section on life style balance.

Is Your Job Right for You?

If you are unhappy with your job, go through the list below and write down all the positive and negative aspects of your job in the same way as you constructed your bulimia balance sheet in chapter 1. It is also worth asking yourself where you want to be in five years' time.

Let's consider Susan's case.

Susan

After leaving school with her A levels, Susan started in a bank on a career training course. Her eating disorder developed during this time, and she became increasingly unhappy. This is her balance sheet in which she considered the options in staying in banking.

1. *Gains and Losses for Myself*
   a. *Positive:* The income is good, and I can get a cheap mortgage.
   b. *Negative:* The work is easy but repetitive and not challenging.
   c. *Negative:* I'm given no freedom or chance to take initiative. School was better than this.
   d. *Positive:* If I stay on, I have a chance of promotion.
   e. *Negative:* With increasing computerisation and world financial changes, opportunities may be limited. Another trainee was rejected during her assessment period.
   f. *Negative:* I spend three hours commuting on overcrowded public transport. I have had to drop out of the local dramatic society and do not have time to go to my St. John Ambulance meetings.
2. *Gains and Losses for Others*
   a. *Positive:* My parents welcome the help with the rent that I can give.
   b. *Positive:* My father likes to tell his friends that I work in the city.
   c. *Negative:* I no longer have time to help in the garden or with our pets.
3. *Self-approval or Disapproval*
   a. *Negative:* I don't like the idea that some of our profits come from lending money to poor countries with questionable leaders.
   b. *Negative:* I resent the fact that all my work is so materialistic—all for profit.

c. *Negative:* I don't use any of the skills I know I have in dealing with people.

d. *Negative:* I can't use any imagination or flair.

e. *Positive:* I would have the opportunity to return to my job if I have children, and the bank would make part-time work available.

4. *Approval or Disapproval from Others*

a. *Positive:* My parents are proud of me working in the city.

b. *Negative:* My friends in the drama society are rather disparaging about my boring city job.

c. *Negative:* I hate it that we are the butt of so much public anger. You constantly have to face customers who are angry that the cash dispenser has gone wrong or that their statement is inaccurate or that they have had to wait too long in the queue.

If there are more stresses, difficulties and minuses than positive things about your job, perhaps it is time to change. Why don't you sit down for a brainstorming session to sort this out.

To make an effective decision about your job, apply the decision making steps used earlier in chapter 2.

Step 1: Define the problem with your current job clearly and concretely.

Step 2: Write down any alternative jobs that you half think you would like to do. This brainstorming requires you to produce ideas without censorship (ignore the voice that says that your father would not approve or that you are bound to fail). Imaginative, wild, and even ridiculous solutions should be included. Quantity rather than quality is important. Later you may need to combine and work on some of these initial ideas.

Step 3: Write down the pros and cons of all the alternative solutions you have produced. For some of the options you have come up with you may need to do some research to find out what is actually involved in a particular job.

Step 4: Rank the available options in terms of your priorities.

You should now be a lot clearer about what you want and what is realistic for you.

FURTHER READING

Back, K., & Back. K. (1982). Assertiveness at work. New York: McGraw Hill.

Edelmann, R.J. *Interpersonal conflicts at work.* Leicester: BPS Books.

Fontana, D. (1993). *Managing time.* Leicester: BPS Books.

Fontana, D. (1990). *Social skills at work.* Leicester: BPS Books.

Is this the End of the Journey—Or Not?

Having worked through this book, ask yourself honestly how you feel. If it has helped you and you are a good step further on your journey towards recovery, excellent! Enjoy the feeling of rest after some hard work. But be prepared for further obstacles along the way. But then, getting better is not about being free of problems—rather, it is about feeling better equipped to deal with them, about feeling more courageous and prepared to try out new things, to look at problems afresh, not to be so trapped by the harsh routines of dieting, the chaos of binges, and the efforts constantly to please others.

BUT WHAT IF YOU ARE STILL STUCK?

If you feel nothing has changed and nothing will ever change, have you actually allowed yourself to work through this book properly? Or have you just rushed through it in a "bingey" sort of fashion and then declared it useless? Maybe you do need to slow down a bit and need to go over it again chapter by chapter. That may seem boring, irritating, tedious, and too difficult to do. Did you know that the people who are most successful in life are the ones who don't give up when they encounter failure? So try again.

DREAM ON, BABY

You may say, "I can't identify with the stories of the women in the book. My problems are different. I can't do anything to change them. Only someone very special can sort them out." It is possible that you are right and that you do need specialist help. But perhaps—and only you can know this—this is just wishful thinking, an excuse, so as to not face the hardships of the journey to recovery.

The Straw that Broke the Camel's Back

Maybe the reason why you haven't been able to change anything is that there are too many things going on in your life that are stressful and difficult, and it feels like you can't juggle all these balls at once.

Go back to the problem-solving chapter (chapter 2) and think again. What is going on in your life that is taking up so much of your time and energies that you can't concentrate on your needs? Is it something to do with your relationships? Is it to do with work? Studies? Your children? Think about it this way: Builders have to do some groundwork before they can start building a house, like clearing the terrain, getting the materials, etc. Without these preparations their task becomes impossible.

Patsy

Patsy was a 50-year-old full-time teacher, who was married with two teenage children. She was also looking after her invalid elderly father in her home. She had to get up several times at night to make sure he was alright and was completely drained by this. She said her husband and children were very supportive. She had in the past also cared devotedly for her mother, until she died three years ago.

She binged several times daily and couldn't understand why this happened. When we gave her this book, she felt that the problems described were not hers. She said that the women in the book were much younger than she, and she felt she had little in common with them. She was very angry about being "lumped in" with people who made themselves sick, which was not one of her problems. In talking to her, it became clear that although her husband and children were sympathetic towards her burden, they actually did very little to help her in practical terms. For example, neither her husband nor her children, who were 13 and 15, did anything in the household. Patsy would go as far as cleaning their shoes and even making sandwiches for everybody to take to school and work. Although Patsy was an extremely bright and well-read woman, she failed to recognise that bingeing was her only way of relieving tension and stress. She had no time for herself and was continuously driven by "shoulds". She experienced reading the book and coming for treatment as further chores and pressures on her, designed to humiliate rather than help her.

If you are a bit like Patsy, try to think of what ground work you have to do, to change your life and allow yourself to concentrate on your eating problem.

RECOVERY: A TRIP INTO UNCHARTED TERRITORY

If you have had an eating disorder for a very long time and it is a very deeply ingrained pattern, changing your habit may be extremely anxiety-provoking, like a journey into the unknown. Or you may fear that if you change a tiny bit, you will set loose an avalanche of change that you then can't contain. Is there really nothing you can do? Perhaps it would be helpful for you to join a self-help group. Find out what is available locally. Or go and talk to your general practitioner. Take the book with you. Tell him or her that you have tried your best to help yourself, but that you need someone to help you to start the journey to recovery properly.

Whatever your story, whatever your outcome, we would like to hear from you. Tell us how you got on with this book, what you found helpful or not so helpful, how you managed to overcome your eating problem, or what stopped you or is still stopping you from overcoming it. You can write to us directly:

Dr. Ulrike Schmidt and Dr. Janet Treasure
Eating Disorder Unit Maudsley Hospital
Denmark Hill
London SE5 8AZ

APPENDIX

Food Diary

Time	What eaten	B	V	L	Antecedents & Consequences

B = Binge, V = Vomited, L = Laxatives

Some Useful Addresses

Alcohol Concern
305 Gray's Inn Road
London WC1X 8QF

AlAnon Family Groups
61 Dover Street
London SE1 4YR
071-403 0888

Alcoholics Anonymous
Head Office
Stonebow House
Stonebow
York YO1 2NJ
0904-644026

British Association for Counselling
37a Sheep Street
Rugby
Warwickshire
W21 3BX
0788-78328/9

Debtors Anonymous
071-328 4802

Eating Disorders Association
Sackville Place
44-48 Magdalen Street
Norwich
Norfolk
0603-621414

National Association of Young People's
Counselling & Advisory Services
17-23 Albion Street
Leicester
LE1 6GD
0533-554775

Relate
Herbert Gray College
Little Church Street
Rugby
Warwickshire
CV21 3AP
0788-73241